GUIDE TO THE BIBLE

Carol Smith

HUMBLECREEK

INSPIRATION FOR LIFE

GUIDE TO THE BIBLE

ISBN 1-58660-479-1

Developed and produced by The Livingstone Corporation.

Interior design by Gary Gnidovic.

Cover design by Robyn Martins.

Page composition by Inside Out Design & Typesetting.

Published by Humble Creek,
P. O. Box 719, Uhrichsville, OH 44683

TABLE OF CONTENTS

3. Where Did the Bible Come From?

Who wrote it? Who compiled it? How did it get to us in the form that it's in?

4. The Basic Anatomy of the Bible

Here's a roadmap for your journey.

5. What Does the Bible Say?

The best way to know what the Bible says is to read it. The next best way is to look at the book-by-book summaries here.

Epilogue

Lists & Stuff

INTRODUCTION

The story of the Bible is the story of God creating the world and then making Himself available to the people of that world. It is a simple straight line from God's heart to ours.

If the Bible sometimes seems difficult to understand, it's because it was written in another culture, at another time, and in another language. Translating it from Greek and Hebrew is no small task. Translating it from ancient culture to our culture can be just as daunting. Both involve understanding the truth as it was significant to that time and culture, then translating that significance to our lives today. In a nutshell, that is one of the great challenges of understanding the Bible and living according to it. Facing that challenge is a large part of what this book is about.

There is another challenge as well. Because the Bible was written in that different place, time, and language it can be easy at times to see it as separate from real life and irrelevant to our lives. On one hand we have the Bible and on the other hand we have everything else. That is far from reality though. The issues that the Bible writers were addressing are still the fundamental issues of life. Where did we come from? Where are we going? How do we survive on the way? How do we relate to our creator? Why do wicked people get ahead? Why is life so unfair? What happens after we die? How can we make a difference in the world? What matters in the big scheme of things?

God addressed all those issues through people who were facing them. He spoke through stories, sermons, songs, poems, visions. . .the very experiences of people who were trying to connect with Him and survive life. What God says to us through those writers is totally relevant to life in any place, time, and language. It's about building a relationship with our creator and facing life within the context of that relationship. It's about understanding that your life fits within a grand scheme, that we are never unheard or unseen, that we are never forgotten. It's understanding God's role within the universe and our place within His heart. It is that very relevance that makes the Bible unique and powerful.

ABBREVIATIONS & DEFINITIONS

Throughout this book you'll see Bible references, for example,
Gen. 1:1

The first part (Gen.) is an abbreviation for a book of the Bible, in this case, Genesis. The number before the colon is a chapter of that book. The number after the colon is a verse within that chapter. On the next page is a list of the books of the Bible with their abbreviations for you to refer to.

You'll notice that some of the books come in installments. In the Old Testament those books were probably written as one book, but fit on two scrolls (like a double video). The second one will be the sequel to the first. In the New Testament the numbered books are letters. So 1 John is the first letter from John that is included. 2 John is yet another letter from John that is included. Get it? They aren't sequels. They are just from the same person. When people talk about the numbered books you'll hear them say, First Samuel, or Second John.

Abbreviations of Bible Books

Most lists of Bible books will be organized in the order that they appear in the Bible. That's not very helpful if you aren't familiar with that order, so some Bibles include an alphabetical list in the upfront information. Here's a list of the books in the order that they appear along with their typical abbreviations. Check back here if you need some clarification. (Yes, you can turn down the corner of the pages. Just don't tell anyone.)

Old Testament

Gen.	Genesis	Eccles.	Ecclesiastes
Exod.	Exodus	Song of Sol.	Song of Solomon
Lev.	Leviticus	Isa.	Isaiah
Num.	Numbers	Jer.	Jeremiah
Deut.	Deuteronomy	Lam.	Lamentations
Josh.	Joshua	Ezek.	Ezekiel
Judg.	Judges	Dan.	Daniel
Ruth	Ruth	Hos.	Hosea
1 Sam.	1 Samuel	Joel	Joel
2 Sam.	2 Samuel	Amos	Amos
1 Kings	1 Kings	Obad.	Obadiah
2 Kings	2 Kings	Jonah	Jonah
1 Chron.	1 Chronicles	Mic.	Micah
2 Chron.	2 Chronicles	Nah.	Nahum
Ezra	Ezra	Hab.	Habakkuk
Neh.	Nehemiah	Zeph.	Zephaniah
Esther	Esther	Hag.	Haggai
Job	Job	Zech.	Zechariah
Ps.	Psalms	Mal.	Malachi
Prov.	Proverbs		

New Testament

Matt.	Matthew	2 Thess.	2 Thessalonians
Mark	Mark	1 Tim.	1 Timothy
Luke	Luke	2 Tim.	2 Timothy
John	John	Titus	Titus
Acts	Acts	Philem.	Philemon
Rom.	Romans	Heb.	Hebrews
1 Cor.	1 Corinthians	James	James
2 Cor.	2 Corinthians	1 Pet.	1 Peter
Gal.	Galatians	2 Pet.	2 Peter
Eph.	Ephesians	1 John	1 John
Phil.	Philippians	2 John	2 John
Col.	Colossians	3 John	3 John
1 Thess.	1 Thessalonians	Jude	Jude
		Rev.	Revelation

Definitions

The Bible: In this book "The Bible" means the modern English Bible made up of sixty-six books (thirty-nine in the Old Testament and twenty-seven in the New Testament). There are other versions of the Bible (such as the Catholic Bible) that may include other books. Some other traditional phrases for the Bible are: Scriptures, Word of God, or God's Word. (You might also hear it referred to as a "sword" because there is a famous verse that refers to it as the sword in our spiritual armor.)

Gospels: the first four books of the New Testament that tell the story of Christ.

Canon: This is a term you might hear used that means the accepted, agreed upon, final list of books that make up the Bible.

Hebrews: Much of the Old Testament centers around the evolution of the Jewish nation. These people can be referred to as the Jews, the Israelites, the children of Israel, the Hebrews, and more. In this book they are usually referred to as the Hebrews.

Holy Land: This is a term used for the land where Jesus lived and worked, particularly the area around Jerusalem.

Passages: A Bible passage is a section. If someone is reading John 1:1–14, then that is the passage he is dealing with. There are not set passages or sections within the Bible like there are chapters and verses. The passage is determined by the study or discussion or reading that you are involved in.

Prophets: Today we often think of prophets as people who tell the future. The prophets of the Bible did have visions of the future but their role in society wasn't so much to tell the future as it was to tell the truth. Their nation's spiritual well-being was in their care and, as God inspired them, they spoke.

Messiah: This is the Old Testament term for Jesus Christ, the one that God promised from the beginning.

Throughout this book you'll find boxes here and there. These boxes contain one of three kinds of information:

IN CONTEXT: How does this piece of the Bible fit in with the whole Bible? What is the context into which it fits?

THINK ABOUT IT THIS WAY: These are organizers for your thoughts. Sometimes we need to see the Bible in light of how it fits into our lives today.

SCRIPTURE BITS: Actual samples of Scriptures

DID YOU KNOW? Facts or concepts that might be new to you

1. The Story of the Bible

The Bible is made up of sixty-six different books, but it's really all one story, a master plan.

THE SHORT VERSION

First, God created an ideal world and put people in it. He gave them the choice to build a relationship with Him or not. Those first people made a mess of things.

Then humanity sort of started all over again. Noah and his family became the only survivors of a worldwide catastrophic flood. Noah's descendants had the same choice, to build a relationship with God or not. Within a few generations, things were in a mess again.

God has remained intent on building a relationship with the people of the world, though. He established a contractlike, covenant agreement with a man named Abraham. Abraham promised to cherish and obey God and to teach his family to do the same. God promised to give Abraham many descendants. God also promised that out of those descendants would come a Messiah, a man who would give His own life on behalf of humanity. That man was God in the form of a human. We refer to Him as Jesus Christ.

Jesus lived and died and lived again. When He left our world, He left behind the message that having a relationship with God requires faith, rather than perfection, on our part. He left behind a group of people who were supposed to keep this message going. He left behind a promise that He would come again, that the world wouldn't always be a broken and disappointing place, that one day all the messes would be cleaned up.

We wait for that time, in faith, trying to keep things as tidy as we can. That's the story of the Bible in short form.

THE NOT-AS-SHORT VERSION

Starting with the Old Testament

The Bible opens with the story of the creation of the world. God created the world and everything in it, including two people, Adam and Eve, and a great garden called Eden. He gave one guideline: Don't eat of this one, certain tree. The importance of that guideline was not the tree, nor what kind of fruit grew on it (which, by the way, probably wasn't an apple). The importance of that guideline was their choice to either walk with God or to walk their own way. From the beginning, God asked people to show their love and devotion through their obedience. Adam and Eve chose to walk their own way. That changed everything.

Adam and Eve had children (remember the Cain and Abel fiasco?), who had children, who had children, and so on. Each generation ignored God more than the generation before. Of Adam and Eve's descendants, one of the most notable was Noah. By the time of Noah, God regretted even making people. (Genesis 6:6) Noah was the one guy of the population who had any concern whatsoever for his relationship with God. God gave humanity another opportunity through Noah. A worldwide flood destroyed everything on earth except the animals and people who moved into Noah's big boat. After the waters receded, the world started over, this time with Mr. and Mrs. Noah, their three sons, and the three sons' wives. (The original *My Three Sons*, pre-Fred MacMurray.)

Noah's children had children, who had children, who had children, and so on, but things didn't get a whole lot better. God gave humanity yet another opportunity, but this time by making a promise kind of agreement with a man named Abraham. God promised He would give Abraham many descendants and that one of those descendants would be the Messiah, the one who would make right this thing that Adam and Eve had messed up. Abraham's part of the promise was that neither he nor his descendants would take their relationship with God lightly and that they would all be circumcised as a sign of their commitment. It was from this agreement that the people we call the Jews or Hebrews descended. The Hebrews are Abraham's descendants.

Abraham had a son, who had twin sons. One of those twins (whose name "Jacob" was changed to "Israel") had twelve sons. Those twelve sons were the patriarchs of the twelve tribes of Israel. They all moved their families to Egypt during a famine, and it was there in Egypt that they began to grow out of an "extended family" and into a "great nation."

Most of the Old Testament is made up of the history of the descendants of these twelve sons. Eventually they became a nation of slaves in Egypt. Through a seeming fluke, a Hebrew baby named Moses escaped slavery and was raised in the king's (Pharaoh's) palace. Moses grew up and led a God-sponsored rebellion, helping his people escape from Egypt. The plan was for Moses to lead his people back to the land that Abraham had settled, way back when. That land was called Israel (after one of Isaac's twin sons), or you might have heard it called "The Promised Land."

IN CONTEXT

The first half (roughly) of the Old Testament is all about God's following through on that promise agreement that He made with Abraham: first in Abraham's backyard, then in Egypt, then in the desert, then in their new land. The rest of the Old Testament really revolves around Israel's struggle to worship God and only God. The historical books describe Israel's struggle with idolatry, then with keeping their land, then with returning to their homes after being taken away as prisoners to other lands. The books of wisdom are the truths that carried them through all those times. The books of prophecy record sermons and visions regarding Israel's unfaithfulness and the bad things that would happen to them because of it. These books also prophesy of the coming Messiah, who would deliver them from their physical and spiritual slavery.

Forty years later, through miracles, mishaps, and misunderstandings, the Hebrews finally reached that land. You may have guessed already that the land had been resettled by other people. Even today there are conflicts in that area about land ownership. Under the leadership of a man named Joshua, the Hebrews set out to reclaim the land. God warned them, actually, to make *everyone else* leave that land. The Hebrews did reclaim much of the land, but they didn't make absolutely everyone leave. That's important to remember.

The reason the Jewish people were supposed to run *everyone else* out of the land is because *everyone else* worshiped idols of some kind. During their travels God had given the Jewish people the Ten Commandments, which began with "You'll have no other gods before me." You know how human nature is. If they let idol worship stay in their land, eventually they would be influenced by it.

And that's e-XACT-ly what happened. The Hebrews kept getting their worship mingled in with the idol worship around them. When they did this, they became weaker and weaker as a nation. As they became weaker (politically and spiritually), they became prey for the surrounding nations. The kingdom divided into two kingdoms. The southern kingdom was Judah and its capital was Jerusalem.

All during this part of Hebrew history, the prophets cried out to their people to turn back to God and let Him protect them from their enemies. But eventually, both the northern and the southern kingdoms of Israel were defeated and taken away from their land into exile. The prophets continued to call out to them even while they were in captivity, asking them to become wholehearted about their relationship with God again. And finally as they started returning and rebuilding, the prophets were there reminding them to keep from making the same mistakes again.

IN CONTEXT

All the way through the Old Testament, from the first time Adam chose his own way to the last time the ancient Jews rebuilt the temple, there was God's promise. The promise always started with an understood, "One day. . ." In the Garden of Eden this promise was to the serpent: One day. . . "he will crush your head" (Genesis 3:15). Later this promise was to Abraham: One day. . . "all peoples on earth will be blessed through you" (Genesis 12:3). Later the promise came through the prophets: One day. . . "the Lord himself will give you a sign: The virgin will be with child and will give birth to a son, and will call him Immanuel" (Isaiah 7:14).

Take a Breath and Review...

All the way through the story so far there was the promise of one coming who would fix what had been broken when people chose their own way rather than God's way. That's what Jesus' life was all about. The Old Testament asked a question: How can we be right with God since we've chosen our own way? The New Testament answered it: through the grace of God given through the life, death, and resurrection of Jesus Christ.

The New Testament

The New Testament opens with the life of Jesus. He was God, having put humanity on so that He could give Himself up for our wrongdoings. He enraged the religious leaders of His day because (1) He claimed to be God and (2) He confronted their hypocrisy and (3) He threatened their authority and power within the community. He said to them in so many words, "God is not about your do's and don'ts. God is about how you live your lives, and connect with Him, and love other people." If they gave up their do's and don'ts, then they didn't have a way to control.

At the age of thirty-three, Jesus was sentenced to death through a true conspiracy instigated by religious leaders. Jesus died as He was hanging on crossbeams of wood. This kind of death was called a crucifixion. It was a painful and agonizing execution typical of that period of history. It was amazing enough that an innocent man was willing to suffer such a death. More amazing than that, while He surely did die on the cross, He came back to life a few days later. He spent some more time with the people He was closest to and then He was gone again, no longer living in a physical body. Before He left the last time, He promised to return again one day to set the record straight once and for all. He also commissioned His followers

IN CONTEXT

The first four books of the New Testament record the events of Jesus' life and ministry. The fifth book records the organization of the early church. The next twenty-one are letters explaining faith and encouraging people and churches. The last book is the prophecy of the end of the world as we know it.

to spread the message of His sacrifice and to love each other along the way.

THINK ABOUT IT THIS WAY

t's like a grocery store coupon. . . .
When people talk about God's plan for keeping us in relationship with Him, they talk about God's redeeming us. They sometimes talk about His plan of redemption. That is really what the big, cohesive plan of the Bible is about—God's process of redeeming us.

Think about it this way. You know those coupons that you (be honest, do you clip coupons?) or somebody you know, clips out of the paper? You take them to the store and you try to buy the things you have coupons for. When you get to the register, you try to remember to show the coupons to the checkout person, then you hope they'll remember to ring them in. If you do remember and they do remember, then what you are doing is REDEEMING those coupons.

In themselves they really aren't worth much. A 2"x3" slick piece of paper is really what they are. Dead tree. But put that manufacturer's seal on them and they're worth something. How much? They're worth whatever the manufacturer says they are worth, that's how much.

God has put into place the necessary scenario for our redemption. He manufactured us. He paid the price—His life. He gave us worth. But we have a part in it. That's why it's not called God's redemption; it's called God's plan for our redemption. He did the work. He made the coupons. He paid the price. He wrote a book to tell us how to get to the right checkout line. He gave no date of expiration. But we have to choose, through faith, to receive the redemption.

It's something to think about next time you're sitting on the floor with sales papers spread out around you and a pair of scissors in your hand.

Those followers became the first missionaries or church-planters. They went to all the surrounding regions spreading the new and exciting message that Jesus had paid the price for our failure to stay in a right relationship with God. They preached grace and faith. They started churches in major cities. Some of them wrote letters back to the churches they had started to help them understand their role in society until Jesus' return.

That's the story of the Bible. It's the story of God's creating us and wooing us into a relationship with Him.

The Old Testament Asked a Question:

How can we be right with God since we've chosen our own way?

The New Testament Answered It:

Through the grace of God given through the life, death, and resurrection of Jesus Christ.

2. A Bible-in-History Lesson

The Bible was written in another time. Understanding that time will help you understand the Bible.

A BIBLE-IN-HISTORY LESSON

Understanding what the Bible means includes understanding the world at the time the Bible was written. Here's a quick history tour.

A TIMELINE

Sometimes we forget that while the events recorded in the Bible were taking place, all the rest of world history was happening as well. We need to understand the biblical events in light of everything that was going on around the world. To add some context, here is a timeline. Keep in mind, there are a lot of differing opinions about the dates. In fact, with a lot of these events, we don't know the exact year. For some, we know of a range that could be as short as three hundred years or as long as one thousand years. In the list below we have often rounded to the nearest century. So, remember the figures we've included are ballpark figures (no, not ballpark franks, ballpark figures).

Around this time . . .	In relation to the Bible . . .	Meanwhile, elsewhere . . .
The beginning of time	God created the world. Adam and Eve begin their family	
8000 B.C.	God saved Noah and his family from the flood. The earth began to repopulate.	
3800 B.C.		A people called the Sumerians moved to Mesopotamia and established their civilization. They built cities including Ur, Abraham's hometown. The Sumerians established arithmetic based on ten (because of the ten fingers they

could count on) and they divided a circle into sixty subsections, setting up the minutes and seconds that we still use today. They also made great gains in the development of writing.

3000 B.C.		The pyramids were built in Egypt.
2500 B.C.		Egyptians discovered papyrus and ink for writing. They built the first libraries.
2250 B.C.		Horses were being domesticated in Egypt and chickens in Babylon.
2000 B.C.	God asked Abraham (who was in Ur) to move to Canaan and promised him that his descendants would have that land. God made Abraham the father of the Jewish nation by giving him Isaac, his son.	Native Americans immigrated to North America from Asia.
1800 B.C.	Joseph, Isaac's grandson, was sold as a slave into Egypt. Eventually his family moved there, too. · The descendants of Joseph and his brothers grew into a nation of slaves in Egypt.	The spoked wheel was invented in the Near East. Egyptian papyrus document describes surgical procedures.
1500 B.C.		The Canaanites invented the first alphabet. Sundials were being used in Egypt.
1400 B.C.	God used Moses to lead the Hebrew people out of Egypt and the slavery there. (This was called the exodus.)	
1350 B.C.	After Moses' death, Joshua led the Hebrews in resettling the land God had promised them—Canaan.	

1300 B.C.	After Joshua's death the Hebrews were ruled by judges, wise men and women who helped settle disagreements and make good choices. Samson and Ruth (of the Bible book by the same name) lived during this time.	Silk fabric invented in China. First Chinese dictionary was forthcoming.
1000 B.C.	God gave Israel their first king: King Saul. Up until this point, Israel was led by wise, religious leaders who made decisions based on spiritual insight. That meant that, ultimately, Israel was led by God (a theocracy). The neighboring nations, though, all had political leaders. The Hebrews basically came to God and said, "We want what the other kids have." After much asking, they got it. Things went out of control from there.	Peking was built.
950 B.C.	Solomon (3rd king) built the temple at Jerusalem.	Celts invade Britain. Assyrians invent inflatable skins (life rafts) for soldiers to cross bodies of water.
900 B.C.	King Solomon died. The kingdom divided into Israel (10 northern tribes, later called Samaria) and Judah (the remaining southern tribes).	
850 B.C.	Elijah rose up as a leader and a prophet among the Hebrews. His successor was Elisha.	
800 B.C.	Isaiah, Joel, Micah, Obadiah, and Nahum prophesied to Judah (the south) while Hosea, Amos, and Jonah prophesied to Israel (the north).	Homer wrote the *Iliad* and the *Odyssey*. Ice skating had become a popular sport in northern Europe.
770 B.C.		The first Olympic Games were held, untelevised, of course.

750 B.C.		Rome became a city. False teeth were invented in Italy shortly after.
650 B.C.		The 33rd Olympics had just introduced horse racing as an event.
600 B.C.	The people of Judah were taken captive into Babylon. The prophets during this time were Jeremiah, Ezekiel, and Daniel.	Japan had just been established as a nation.
550 B.C.		Siddhartha Gautama, founder of Buddhism, was born. Aesop just wrote his fables. Confucius was born in China. The lock and key and carpenter's square were invented.
500 B.C.	The first Israelite exiles returned to Jerusalem and began to rebuild.	At the same time in Greece, Pythagoras, a mathematician, discovered that the square of the hypotenuse of a right-angled triangle is equal to the sum of the squares of the other two sides. (Remember the Pythagorean Theorem in geometry?) Halloween originated in a Celtic festival. An Indian surgeon performs the first known cataract operation.
450 B.C.	The rebuilding of the temple in Jerusalem was complete. The ruler at this time was Cyrus the Persian. The Jewish leadership was Ezra and Nehemiah. The prophets were Haggai and Zechariah.	Around the same time (within a decade or so) Hippocrates was born. He grew up to be the "Father of Medicine" (remember the Hippocratic oath?) and wrote the oldest medical books that still exist. He taught the world that sickness comes from physical causes rather than superstitions or evil.
447 B.C.		The Parthenon was built in Athens.
427 B.C.		Plato was born in Greece.

425 B.C.	Queen Esther was crowned in Persia (a Jewish queen of Persia?).	
399 B.C.		Socrates died.
300 B.C.		Alexander the Great established his empire. Aristarchos stated that the earth rotates on an axis and is not the center of the universe.
250 B.C.	The Septuagint was translated. This was a Greek translation of the OT. Greek was the common language of that time so this was a BIG deal. Jesus and His disciples probably used this translation.	Meanwhile, Erastitratos discovered that the brain, instead of the heart, was the center of nerve activity.
150 B.C.	A dad and five brothers led a revolt (the Maccabean revolt) against an evil Syrian ruler. Judas, the eldest son, led the Jewish nation into a time of prosperity.	Meanwhile, Eratosthenes, a mathematician, correctly calculated the circumference of the earth.
50 B.C.		Julius Caesar was assassinated and Augustus Caesar became the new Roman ruler (he is the official who ordered the census that caused Joseph and the very pregnant Mary to travel to Bethlehem, where Jesus was born). Meanwhile, in Greece, the first steam engine was being envisioned. Also, in Rome, Marcus Vitruvius, an architect, wrote a book on city planning including clocks, hydraulics, and military engines. In Phoenicia, glass-blowing was invented.
		Cleopatra becomes ruler.
30 B.C.		Cleopatra and Mark Antony commit

suicide. Sumo wrestling was about to rise to the forefront in Japan.

Beginning of A.D. time	Jesus is born around this time, but probably actually around 5 B.C. Some things are not perfect in hindsight.	
A.D. 30	Jesus of Nazareth was crucified (assassinated) and miraculously returned to life. After He returned to heaven, the Holy Spirit arrived at a time that we now call "Pentecost."	
A.D. 60	Paul wrote his early letters to the churches.	Romans begin using soap. Meanwhile, Celsus, a medical writer, suggested using antiseptics on wounds.
A.D. 65	Mark's Gospel, then Matthew's Gospel, then Luke's Gospel and Acts were written.	At the same time, Rome was partly burned, which prompted Nero to blame and persecute Christians. Somewhere, artists began painting on canvas.
A.D. 70	Jerusalem was destroyed again.	
A.D. 80		Mt. Vesuvius erupted in Italy, burying Pompeii.
A.D. 85	John's Gospel was written. Paul made his missionary journeys.	Wang Chung, a Chinese philosopher, declared that any theory must be supported by concrete evidence and experimental proof. (This was the birth of the scientific method at the same time that the greatest miracle of all time was being spread through the civilized world.)
A.D. 90	Individual churches started sharing Paul's letters with each other.	
A.D. 100	The four Gospels were circulated together as a collection.	At the same time Archigenes, a doctor who was reputed to be the first dentist, made the inaugural drill into a human tooth (while still attached to a living human being). Unfortunately, novocaine had not been invented yet. Meanwhile, the Roman Empire was at the height of its power.

A.D. 120	All thirteen of Paul's letters were pulled together as a collection. (We now call these the Pauline Epistles.)	
A.D. 140	A man named Marcion put together a Bible that rejected the Old Testament and and rewrote a lot of the New Testament. This motivated the church leaders to make a decision to recognize officially what books made up the New Testament Canon.	
A.D. 145	The church stood against Marcion and recognized all the books of the New Testament. This Testament was almost identical to ours.	
A.D. 150		Galen, a surgeon to the gladiators in Pergamum, discovered that human arteries carry blood and not air, as was generally assumed.
A.D. 400	An official council acknowledged what had already been proven as people experienced the power of God's Word: The twenty-seven books that we know today as the New Testament were true and inspired by God.	

GEOGRAPHY

Most of the story of the Bible takes place around the eastern shores of the Mediterranean Sea. If you have a map, find Africa. In the northeasternmost corner, you'll find Egypt. Let your finger follow the shoreline eastward up and around and you'll find Israel. Israel was Abraham's home, called Canaan. Later it was called the Promised Land for the Hebrews who were set free from Egypt. If you continue on up around the shoreline, you'll find Greece. This is the path covered by much of Paul's missionary journeys, even as far as Rome, Italy.

Today we can travel across oceans and continents in the course of a day. It's hard to imagine that so much of the history of the Bible happened in a relatively small space of land. This points out, too, the beauty of God's timing, entering humanity at a time when the hub of the world was small and the good news could disseminate worldwide very quickly and easily.

That's the big picture. Let's get more specific. Here are the places that the people whom you read about in the Bible encountered as they walked through their everyday lives.

Houses and Homes

During the Old Testament days, most people traveled with their flocks and herds, so the most common homes were tents made of poles, stakes, and skins. Curtains divided the tents into rooms and rugs covered the ground inside. The sides of the tents could be folded back to create porches and let fresh air circulate. This was community in a way we hardly recognize with our brick homes and "Close the windows! The air's on!"

As cultures became more stable, they began to build small homes inside of courtyards. Compared to our standards, the homes were small and cramped but held entire families. Occasionally they had separate rooms but seldom doors to the rooms. Usually the homes were made of stone, but near the Jordan they were also made with bricks made of river mud and baked in the sun. The roofs were often beams with brush laid across them.

As time went by, the Hebrews built four-room homes. This structure allowed the builders to build a sturdy roof and then to utilize that roof as a porch or sitting area. Either an outside staircase or even just a ladder led to the upper level.

In New Testament times, Middle Eastern homes were built of mud bricks, usually on a stone or limestone foundation. Outside, staircases led to flat roofs that provided a sitting area and extra storage space. Small windows allowed airflow but kept out intruders. Most houses had a small raised area for sleeping. Only wealthier people had upper rooms, courtyards, or gardens.

Whether the homes held rich families or poor families, they typically had much less furniture than we use today. Instead of couches, people often sat on mats and cushions. Instead of tables, they had circular pieces of leather. Instead of bed frames, they had mattresses. Instead of candles and electric lamps, they had oil lamps.

SCRIPTURE BITS

House Rules

"Every new house you build must have a barrier around the edge of its flat rooftop. That way you will not bring the guilt of bloodshed on your household if someone falls from the roof."

Deuteronomy 22:8 NLT

One day Elisha went to the town of Shunem. A wealthy woman lived there, and she invited him to eat some food. From then on, whenever he passed that way, he would stop there to eat. She said to her husband, "I am sure this man who stops in from time to time is a holy man of God. Let's make a little room for him on the roof and furnish it with a bed, a table, a chair, and a lamp. Then he will have a place to stay whenever he comes by."

2 Kings 4:8–10 NLT

Tabernacles, Temples, and Synagogues

Church buildings are not as important in our communities as they once were, yet we see them everywhere. The phrase "a church on every corner" still translates well in a lot of western civilization. Religious buildings were far more important in ancient time, but were not so ever-present.

Before God's people reached the Promised Land, they wandered in the desert for many years. Because of their nomadic lifestyle, they needed a portable place of worship. A tent, also called the tabernacle, served the purpose. It was the only "church building" in the Jewish camp. It was considered the place where God dwelled.

After the Israelites had settled in the Promised Land and enjoyed a time of peace, King Solomon built the grand temple his father David had envisioned. It was a permanent place for the people to worship God and offer sacrifices. The temple was based on the plans of the tabernacle. There was an inner room called the Holy of Holies. This place was reserved for God's very presence. The ark of the covenant (a sacred box with some artifacts from the miracles on their journey) was placed there as well.

There were some other worship centers established, partly, for people who lived far away from Jerusalem. They needed places closer to home to offer their sacrifices. The temple at Jerusalem was the preferred location, though. At least once a year most people traveled there. You might remember when Mary and Joseph took Jesus to the temple in Jerusalem to celebrate the Passover and got separated from each other. (Luke 2:41–47)

In the New Testament, local synagogues were the mainstay of biblical instruction. Synagogues may have actually begun as early as during the Hebrew exile in Babylon. Because the people could not return to the temple to worship, they may have begun gathering together to study and encourage each other.

DID YOU KNOW?

The Order of a Synagogue Service

During a service at a synagogue, the women sat on one side of the room and the men sat on the other. The services usually began with a creed of confession. Often it was from Deuteronomy 6:4–5.

> Hear, O Israel: The LORD our God, the LORD is one. Love the LORD your God with all your heart and with all your soul and with all your strength.
>
> (Deuteronomy 6:4–5)

The service included prayers and Scripture readings (from several different sections of Scripture) and then an instructional sermon. There was often a time of question and answer after that. In many liturgical church services today, you can still see the elements of the synagogue service.

The actual structure of the synagogues varied. They often reflected the community that built them in terms of how elaborately they were built and decorated. Each synagogue would have included at least a chest for the scrolls (like the table with the Bible in front of traditional western churches), a platform for the teacher, musical instruments, and benches for the learners. Sounds a little familiar, doesn't it?

FOOD

Keep in mind that this was not a world of meat packaged in cellophane and aisle after aisle of canned foods. This was a time when variety was not at a premium. People often grew their own food. When they shopped, it was at open-air markets. There was no refrigeration, so meat was often cured with salt and dried (like jerky). Spices were not the everyday items that we find in our cupboards today, but some common spices were dill, mustard, and mint. Sugar was not even present.

Typically, a Hebrew breakfast was lighter than a PopTart. It was usually a snack eaten during the course of the tasks of the morning—maybe a piece of bread or fruit. Lunch was light, maybe some bread and olives or fruit. The evening meal was the largest. A family with a modest income probably sat together sharing a big bowl of vegetable stew. Instead of spoons, they probably dipped their bread into the pot to eat. In richer homes the meals may have been enjoyed in courses with pastries or fruit for dessert.

For beverages there were no pop-top soda cans or cream soda. The water wasn't even always safe for drinking. (No, there was no bottled water.) They probably had goat milk, fresh juice, or wine with meals.

In short, there was no kid standing in front of the fridge, door wide open, looking for something to microwave. Foods were blander, coarser, and less varied. Meals were more trouble to make and store. And probably people were a lot more grateful for the food they ate than in the middle-class western world.

Popcorn and Figs

On a wider view, grain was the universal food source in Bible times. In fact, grain was so valuable, it was often used as money. While the men planted, tended, and harvested the crops, the women and children worked to prepare the family's meals. For example, grain seeds needed to be sorted to remove any poisonous kernels; then they were either popped on a hot griddle or ground into cornmeal to make flat cakes.

Grapes, olives, and figs were also abundant in Bible times. Grapes were crushed and fermented for drinking. Olives were crushed for their oil, which was used for cooking, cleaning, lighting, and medicinal purposes. Figs added a variety to people's diets. Believe it or not, for a snack, Hebrews sometimes ate locusts, crickets, or grasshoppers (not chocolate-covered, either).

Here are some interesting facts about the Hebrew diet:

- Honey was the main sweetener. There was no sugar.

- Butter was hardly used (because of preservation), but cheese and yogurt were very popular.

- Vegetables were often eaten raw.

- The most common kind of bread was in flat cakes rather than loaves (pita-like).

A Kosher Diet

You've heard of "keeping kosher." The original guidelines for a kosher diet actually came during the Hebrew's exodus out of Egypt. Moses gave them God's guidelines for a healthy diet. The guidelines included things like:

- When eating meat, use this rule of thumb: Eat only animals that chew their cud and have divided hooves. (That leaves out pork, no cud-chewing, and camels, no divided hooves.)
- As for animals that live in the sea, eat only fish with fins and scales (so no turtles or clams or octopus or crab or even scallops).
- Whatever you eat, the blood should be drained from the carcass before cooking.
- Don't cook or eat meat and milk dishes together.
- Don't eat fat.

The list of forbidden food included camels, rabbits, badgers, pigs, reptiles, and certain birds, including eagles, vultures, falcons, owls, and bats. These dietary laws protected a huge group of travelers from disease.

FASHION

No Name Brands

Today we have different kinds of clothes for different occasions. We have sports clothes, casual clothes, work clothes, dress casual work clothes, dressy clothes, formal clothes, and so on. Men wear ties for some events and T-shirts for others. Women wear high heels for some events and flip-flops for others. We have a lot of variety in the kinds of clothes we wear. It wasn't that way in the time when the Bible was written. The difference between fancy and casual was just a matter of color and decorative accessories. That was also the difference between the clothes of the wealthy and the clothes of the poor.

As you can imagine, a lot of the fashion decisions from 4,000 B.C. until A.D. 400 were determined by weather. The climate around the Mediterranean Sea was hot and dry with full sun exposure. We look at pictures of their long robes and think, *How hot! I'd rather wear shorts!* We forget that their clothes served to shade them from a fierce, full sun. The color of their clothes repelled the sun, but the weave of the cloth let air pass through. It was the time of the original natural fibers.

There was one thing about the Hebrew wardrobe that was similar to today. You could often tell a person's occupation from the clothes he or she wore. For example, priests wore special gowns and rabbis wore blue-fringed robes.

Don't Leave Home Without It

The most basic item of clothing for both men and women was a tunic. The tunic was covered with a long, wool garment called a cloak. Most people owned only one cloak at a time. They were expensive and time-consuming to make. A cloak was a valuable and versatile possession. It was a blanket to sit on, a carry-all bag, bedding on cool nights, and even a pledge for a debt. In Exodus a law was passed down that a person's cloak should always be returned before nightfall. It was an important item—sometimes it meant a person's survival.

A Trip to the Mall

The Men's Shop

No, there weren't really malls in Bible times. But if Peter or John had gone to a mall to buy a wardrobe, these are the kinds of items you'd see on the racks.

Loincloths: not so fitting as even boxers, they still performed the same function.

Inner tunics: like an undershirt made of cotton or linen. They were thigh-length or ankle-length and were generally for cooler weather.

Tunic coats: This was the basic. It was worn more than any other garment. Most tunics fit about as closely as modern day shirts. They were often long-sleeved, floor-length, and solid colored. Working men or slaves sometimes wore knee-length, without sleeves (think of the messenger in a Roman centurion movie). Very important men wore all white.

Girdles: No, not for tummies. They were cloth or leather belts worn over the tunic coat. They were usually two to six inches wide and sometimes were studded with iron, silver, or gold. When cloth girdles were tied in the back, they functioned as a belly-pack in front to carry small items like a snack or loose change.

Cloaks, mantles, or robes: These were large, loose-fitting garments that were worn over everything else. For the working man, a cloak was made of wool, goat hair, or camel hair. For an upper-crust guy, a cloak would be made of linen, wool, velvet, or silk and could be elaborately bordered and lined with fur.

The headdresses: There were usually three varieties: the cap (brimless cotton or wool), the turban (thick linen scarf or sash wound around the head, concealing the ends), and the headscarf (square yard of cotton, wool, or silk draped around the head and held in place by several silk twists. No baseball caps and no visors.

Sandals or shoes: Shoes were made of soft leather in a moccasin kind of style. Sandals were made of a rougher, more durable leather.

Accessories: nose rings, rings. (Yes, on guys. Yes, before alternative music.)

Best-Dressed Women

If Mary or Martha had stopped by a boutique, these are the items they would find hanging on the rounders. The pieces had the same function as the men's clothes, but they were made to look feminine with embroidery and needlework.

Tunics: Ladies' tunics were always ankle-length. They often had fringe at the bottom with a sash of silk or wool.

Headdresses: Mary's headdress would have been a lot different from Peter's. Mary's would have probably been a small, stiff cap fastened with spangles and a thin veil to cover most of her face.

Undergarments: Yes, they had them, though not in so many styles as today. What kind of fabric a woman wore had a lot to do with her status. The choices were usually cotton, linen, or silk.

Gowns: Ladies' gowns were often floor-length with pointed sleeves (precursors to the Cinderella-type sleeves).

Petticoats: This was a small jacket sporting fine needlework. (Are you thinking I Dream of Jeanie? She often wore something like this.)

Accessories: One thing is the same. Ladies had a lot more options on accessories than men did. Maybe that's because men turned their attention more to racing their camels. Ladies' accessories included earrings (also called chains, pendants), nose rings, anklets (spangles), bracelets, and elaborately braided hair.

SOCIETY

Gender Roles

This might hurt a bit, ladies, but the Bible reflects a culture in which women didn't really have full rights as people. They were not even considered reliable witnesses in legal matters. Often when you read an account of a crowd in the Bible, you will just be given the number of men in the crowd. (That can make the event even more amazing when you add in women and children. Matthew 14:19–21) Basically, in Bible times, men were trained for farming, hunting, and fighting in wars. Women typically tended the children and cared for the needs of the home.

There were exceptions, though. Deborah was a judge (Judges 4:4). Miriam was a worship leader (Exodus 15:20). Anna was a prophetess (Luke 2:36).

When you understand the typical role of women in the ancient world, then you understand how revolutionary Jesus' life and ministry was. He honored women as people (John 4:7–9). He allowed them to minister alongside Him and even support Him in His ministry (Luke 8:1–3). Today, when women still struggle against gender stereotypes, Jesus' style would be refreshing. In the time in which He lived, it was downright radical!

Servants

The ancient world described in the Bible had more than its share of barbarism. You can be sure of that. Prisoners of war were often horribly mistreated, tortured, and killed. If they weren't killed, then they were probably taken into slavery. The kind of treatment they received as slaves was probably dependent upon the ruler of that time. When the Israelites were slaves in Egypt, they were given impossible tasks and ill-treated (Exodus 1:11–14). But every time that slavery is mentioned in the Bible, it does not have the connotations of cruelty and inhumane treatment.

Slavery in ancient days was often a way to pay off debt. In fact, a person could choose to sell himself as a slave to change his financial situation. There was also a system in place for a slave to choose to become a lifelong slave. This often happened because he or she was happy in his or her place in life and chose it almost like we would choose a career today.

The quality of a slave's life depended almost entirely on the nationality and character of his master. Roman law decreed that slaves were the legal property of their master, giving Roman masters complete control and authority over their servants. Jewish law provided slaves with limited rights, although they were still expected to obey their masters. Scripture required Jewish people to grant their Hebrew slaves freedom in the seventh year and a special year of celebration known as the Jubilee Year (Leviticus 25:39–42; Deuteronomy 15:12). Most slaves were forced to do manual labor, but some were nurses, tutors, and even doctors. In fact, some educated people would sell themselves into slavery for a limited period of time to acquire Roman citizenship.

IN CONTEXT

The whole book of Philemon in the New Testament is rooted in a slavery scenario. A slave named Onesimus ran away from his master and then became a Christian. The Book of Philemon is actually a letter of commendation that the apostle Paul wrote to accompany Onesimus as he returned to his master, Philemon. While Paul taught over and over again that we are free in Christ, slavery, as a societal role, was an accepted part of that culture.

Marriages and Mistresses

To the modern female mind, the concept of concubines can be quite hard to take.

A concubine was a woman who became a part of a household in much the way a wife would. The husband and head of the house assumed the obligations of a husband to this woman, but she didn't have the rights and privileges of a wife. She was responsible for part of the household. She bore children by her "husband," and her sons had the same right to inheritance as the sons of the wives. She couldn't be sold away or gotten rid of, but she was always a concubine rather than a wife.

In the Bible, polygamy (having more than one wife) and concubines are mentioned as a matter of course. It's important to note, though, that the Bible also lists the negative outcomes of households with multiple wives and concubines. It was not a happy or healthy arrangement.

The story of Sarah and Hagar in Genesis 16 is a powerful example. Sarah gave her Egyptian slave, Hagar, to her husband, Abraham, to bear children for her. In that day, giving substitute wives for childbearing was a common practice, even a requirement. (Having children was the ultimate accomplishment and purpose for a woman in those days. It was a shame for her not to give her husband any kids, particularly sons. It was a greater shame than giving him another woman.) After Hagar served as a surrogate mother and bore Abraham a son, Sarah mistreated and abused her because she was jealous of her ability to conceive. Hagar's son, Ishmael, fathered the Arab nation. Sarah's son, Isaac, fathered the Jewish nation. If you watch the news, you know that conflicts between the two continue even to this day (Genesis 16:1–12).

Some kings in ancient times had so many concubines that they built a separate building for them near the palace called a harem. The harem was filled with young virgins taken from their homes for one reason—to serve the king and fulfill his sexual needs. Some of these women lived in the harem all of their lives, only to be summoned by the king once. In the Book of Esther, you'll read the story of a young Jewish girl who became part of the harem of a Persian king named Xerxes (Esther 2:7–17).

King Solomon was famous for his seven hundred wives and three hundred concubines. He often married foreign princesses to build political alliances with surrounding nations. Because of that, they influenced him to worship their foreign gods. This led to the downfall of his kingdom and his faith.

War and Prejudice

The accounts in the Old Testament describe a world that is war-filled and barbaric. Sometimes as a reader you can feel like you're reading the stories of Conan the Barbarian or the Klingons in *Star Trek*. The truth is that the ancient world was full of mutual hatred and intense rivalries. The globe that would fit that time had no set boundaries drawn in. Land was always up for grabs. "Conquer or be conquered" was the law of the land.

Longtime enemies of Israel included the Philistines, Assyrians, Ammonites, and Egyptians. As you read through historical accounts, as well as the Psalms and the prophets, you'll find these enemies listed over and over again. It was not a "love your enemy" kind of time. It was an "eye for an eye" kind of time. Much of the story of the Old Testament has to do with God's preserving that family line through which Jesus would come. Jesus would then inaugurate a new way of living that had the potential to put war and prejudice away completely. To preserve that family line often meant battle lines were drawn. The Bible tells of some amazing and miraculous victories. The Hebrews also suffered severe defeats.

Even in the New Testament, you'll read about the hatred Jewish people had for Samaritans. Major racial tension. Here's the history—when the Assyrians invaded the northern kingdom of Israel in 722 B.C., they deported many foreigners to settle there. Over time, the Jewish people and Assyrians intermarried, creating a mixed race called the Samaritans. "Pure-bred" Jewish people from the southern kingdom refused to associate with Samaritans because they considered them "half-breeds." Understanding this piece of history gives you more of an understanding of the parable of the Good Samaritan (Luke 10:29–37), as well as Jesus' boldness in talking with the Samaritan woman at the well (John 4:7–9).

THE JOB MARKET

Employment Opportunities

The days described in the Old Testament were mostly agricultural. In New Testament times, both agricultural industries and service industries began to organize. Importing and exporting were a part of the trade. Much like today, cities produced livelier trade and more career options than villages and small towns. Also, cities that were built around ports or trade routes had a greater variety and more accomplished technology. Here's a list of descriptions from the job market in the Middle East during Bible times.

SCRIPTURE BITS

Career Day

Lamech [Cain's great-great-great grandson] married two women—Adah and Zillah. Adah gave birth to a baby named Jabal. He became the first of the herdsmen who live in tents. His brother's name was Jubal, the first musician—the inventor of the harp and flute. To Lamech's other wife, Zillah, was born Tubal-cain. He was the first to work with metal, forging instruments of bronze and iron.

Genesis 4:19–22 NLT

Farmers

As early as the fourth chapter of Genesis, farming was a way of survival. In fact, when God banished Adam and Eve from the Garden, He told them that they would find their food in the ground and that it would be hard work.

And to Adam [God] said, "Because you listened to your wife and ate the fruit I told you not to eat, I have placed a curse on the ground. All your life you will struggle to scratch a living from it. It will grow thorns and thistles for you, though you will eat of its grains. All your life you will sweat to produce food, until your dying day. Then you will return to the ground from which you came. For you were made from dust, and to the dust you will return." (Genesis 3:17–19 NLT)

Through Old Testament history, most peasant families supported themselves through farming. After the fall rains, when the soil was soft, farmers used wooden plows to prepare the dirt for planting. Seeds were hand-scattered, then farmers depended on steady spring rains to bring the crops. They harvested by pulling out whole plants by hand or by using a wooden sickle to cut the grain stalks. The husks were separated from the grain on the threshing floor, a hard, smooth area outside of the house. A large, forked tool was used in the winnowing process to toss the grain into the air, allowing the evening wind to blow away the chaff. The quality grain left was measured and prepared for meals in the home or for sale in the village market.

It was in this kind of setting that Ruth met Boaz (Ruth 2:1–3) and that God called Gideon to be a leader of Israel (Judges 6:11).

Fishermen

During Old Testament times, the Israelites were often wandering from home to home, like nomads in the desert. They did not depend heavily on fishing. But by the time of the New Testament, the people were settled in their land and there was a flourishing fishing industry around the Sea of Galilee. Fish were so abundant that some fishermen stood on the shores, threw out a circle of netting (weighted around the edges), and pulled in a good catch of fish. Most fisherman, however, used boats to take them farther out into the lake. Often, a net with weights on the bottom and corks on the top would be thrown out between two fishing boats and dragged to shore.

Bible stories tell us a lot about the fishing business during this time. Sometimes fishermen worked all night at their job (John 21:3–4). Some of the greatest dangers of fishing were the unpredictable storms on the Sea of Galilee (Matthew 8:23–27). Simon Peter and his brother Andrew were career fishermen before becoming disciples of Christ (Matthew 4:18–19).

> *One day as Jesus was walking along the shores of the Sea of Galilee, he saw Simon and his brother, Andrew, fishing with a net, for they were commercial fishermen. Jesus called out to them, "Come, be my disciples, and I will show you how to fish for people!" And they left their nets at once and went with him.* (Mark 1:16–18 NLT)

Artisans and Craftsmen

"He will be able to create beautiful workmanship from gold, silver, and
bronze; he can cut and set stones like a jeweler, and can do beautiful carv-
ing; in fact, he has every needed skill. And God has made him and Oholiab
gifted teachers of their skills to others. (Oholiab is the son of Ahisamach, of
the tribe of Dan.) God has filled them both with unusual skills as jewelers,
carpenters, embroidery designers in blue, purple, and scarlet on linen back-
grounds, and as weavers—they excel in all the crafts we will be needing in
the work." (Exodus 35:32–35 TLB)

From almost the beginning of the Bible, craftsmen were recognized. A
craftsman among the Hebrews was someone who supported his family by
producing crafts and artifacts to sell. Today we value things that are "hand-
made." In those days, that was everything!

Potters were in great demand. Copper containers were often expensive
and leather hide bottles (like those used for wine) couldn't be used for
everything. So clay or earthenware pottery was essential. Potters made clay
cooking and eating utensils. A Hebrew potter probably kneaded the clay
with his feet, then molded it into various shapes of vessels on his potting
wheel.

Woe to those who try to hide their plans from God, who try to keep him in
the dark concerning what they do! "God can't see us," they say to themselves.
"He doesn't know what is going on!" How stupid can they be! Isn't he, the
Potter, greater than you, the jars he makes? Will you say to him, "He didn't
make us"? Does a machine call its inventor dumb? (Isaiah 29:15–16 TLB)

Carpenters made plows, winnowing forks, and threshing tools for farming, as well as roofs, doors, window frames, and furniture for homes. They
used tools such as saws, awls, and hammers. Sometimes carpenters worked
with metal and stone as well as wood. Joseph, Jesus' earthly father, was a
carpenter and Jesus was known to His neighbors as a carpenter.

"He's just the carpenter, the son of Mary and brother of James, Joseph, Judas,
and Simon. And his sisters live right here among us." (Mark 6:3 NLT)

Tanners fashioned cowhide and goatskin and the hides of other animals into sandals, bags, tents, shields, flooring, and water sacks. Because tanners worked with animals that were considered unclean, the trade was scorned and tanners were often required to work outside of the city. Tanners often used bone tools to scrape the hides. They used lime and bark from certain trees to tan the skins. The Bible mentions that Peter stayed with a tanner named Simon when he was in Joppa.

Masons worked in stone. They molded and shaped limestone rocks to be used in construction. They built walls and foundations. Their tools included a plumb line (an ancient vertical level), a measuring reed, and a variety of hammers and chisels. The prophet Amos, among others, used the mason's plumb line as an example of God's judgment of the faithfulness of Israel.

Other craftsmen included **coppersmiths, goldsmiths, silversmiths,** and **weavers.**

Herdsmen

Herdsmen were the sharecroppers of livestock. They often did not own the animals that they tended, but their pay was in the form of products from the herd. Herdsmen tended to oxen, sheep, goats, and camels. Theirs was an honorable profession. Probably the most prominent herdsmen in the Bible were the shepherds.

Shepherds were usually responsible for a flock of sheep and goats mixed together. Their tasks included feeding the flock, leading it to green pastures, protecting the animals from wild animals, and keeping track of the flock. Shepherds sometimes had to travel far with their herds to find pastures, especially in the hot summer months.

Both goats and sheep were valuable: goats for milk, meat, and their hair, which was used to make clothing, and sheep for their wool and meat.

In the Bible you will find the role of the shepherd used over and over again as a metaphor for God's care for us. About God, Isaiah wrote,

He tends his flock like a shepherd: He gathers the lambs in his arms and carries them close to his heart; he gently leads those that have young. (Isaiah 40:11)

David wrote,

The LORD is my shepherd, I shall not be in want. (Psalm 23:1 NIV)

Jesus even said,

"I am the good shepherd; I know my sheep and my sheep know me— just as the Father knows me and I know the Father—and I lay down my life for the sheep." (John 10:14–15 NIV)

To the modern world these comparisons are poetic and beautiful. To the ancient world they were familiar and understandable. There was a direct connection to their everyday lives.

Priests

There were two different kinds of workers in the temple. The Levites were responsible for the upkeep of the temple and the operations. Levites were descendants of Levi, one of the twelve sons of Israel (and the tribe that Moses descended from).

Moses' brother, Aaron, was the first high priest. The priests in the temple all descended from his particular bloodline in the Levite tribe. (Talk about needing a census.) The office of priest was established by God to mediate between God and the nation of Israel. Priests were responsible to help the common people maintain a right relationship with God, as well as to oversee the everyday operations of the temple and maintain the system of daily sacrifices.

Though this is a very loose comparison, the closest comparison to the modern Protestant church would be this: The Levites would include all the church staff and particularly those who handle the administration and upkeep of the church and its buildings. The priests would be those of the church staff who handle worship and the spiritual development of the people of the church.

The book of Hebrews compares Jesus' role in our lives to that of a high priest.

Therefore, it was necessary for Jesus to be in every respect like us, his brothers and sisters, so that he could be our merciful and faithful High Priest before God. He then could offer a sacrifice that would take away the sins of the people. (Hebrews 2:17 NLT)

That is why we have a great High Priest who has gone to heaven, Jesus the Son of God. Let us cling to him and never stop trusting him. This High Priest of ours understands our weaknesses, for he faced all of the same temptations we do, yet he did not sin. (Hebrews 4:14–15 NLT)

Just a Few More...

Here are a few more common occupations listed in the Bible:

- **Bakers:** made bread or baked dough that customers brought in (Genesis 40:1)

- **Barbers:** cut hair, most often worked on the street (Ezekiel 5:1)

- **Counselors or advisors:** advised the king or another official (1 Chronicles 27:32)

- **Diviners:** seemed to have access to secret knowledge, particularly future events (1 Samuel 6:2)

- **Dyers:** extracted color from natural sources and dyed cloth (2 Chronicles 2:7)

- **Elders:** were chief men or magistrates of the cities (Genesis 23:10)

- **Merchants:** imported and made merchandise available for sale to the public (Luke 19:45)

- **Nurses:** acted as tutors, guides, foster parents, or nannies (Genesis 24:59)

- **Perfumers:** dealt with anything fragrant, including apothecary as well as cosmetic items (1 Samuel 8:13)

- **Physicians:** understood and practiced the art of healing (Jeremiah 8:22)

- **Scribes:** handled correspondence, kept accounts, and transcribed documents (Ezra 7:6)

- **Politicians:** held positions as rulers, senators, magistrates, anyone involved in government (1 Chronicles 23:2)

- **Singers:** functioned as trained or professional vocalists (1 Chronicles 15:27)

- **Soldiers:** held rank in professional military service (Judges 9:4)

- **Tax collectors:** gathered taxes for the Roman government (Matthew 9:9)

CHURCH HISTORY 101

The political and social world of the Bible was very different than our modern world. The world of the church was different as well.

There's a church on every block in many Western cities. There are small churches and big churches and loads of different denominations. As they grow, they often add buildings to their campuses. Sometimes they build gyms or family life centers. They add libraries. They clear off softball fields.

That is nothing like the early church. In fact, the early church had nothing to do with buildings at all. The early church was just the people who believed in Jesus and the miracle of His resurrection. They were identified by the cities they lived in. They united to spread the news and to encourage each other. They didn't meet because it was what they always did. They met because they needed each other. They didn't have buildings. In fact, during times of persecution, a church building would have been the most dangerous place to be.

When you read the books in the New Testament that are letters (called epistles), you realize that most of the churches were called by their city names. The Ephesian church was all the believers in Ephesus. The Philippian church was all the believers in Philippi. They hadn't divided into denominations. They were just the followers of Christ who were willing to admit their faith and join together to continue Jesus' ministry. You've probably heard ministers today encourage the modern church to become more like the New Testament church in this way.

The Ministry

What do you think of when you think of someone who is "in the ministry"? Do you think of clerical collars? Hospital visits? Preaching from pulpits? Church offices?

Today we often think of a pastor who goes to one church for a while, then goes to another church, probably in the same denomination. That church pays him a salary and probably provides some kind of benefits package.

Ministry for the prophets of the Old Testament and the early church leaders of the New Testament was a whole different thing. They were most often "itinerant," which was like being a freelance pastor who traveled around to different congregations. They were often in a dangerous profession. They withstood persecution. Often there were other religions in their area that were as fervent in their beliefs if not more so. There were no salary packages or benefits. The pastors and teachers depended on the people of the congregation to sustain them. Many, such as the apostle Paul, were bivocational, which means they had a day job (like tent-making) that they used to support themselves so they could minister in their off time.

CURRENCIES, WEIGHTS, AND MEASUREMENTS

For all of our societal evolution, two things about the marketplace are the same now as they were in the days described in the Bible:

1. Shoppers wanted to get the most for their money, and
2. Merchants wanted to get paid well for their products/services.

Because of this, from the beginning of civilization, money and measurements were developing into standard systems.

It is difficult to imagine a world like the early Old Testament world in which standard weights or measurements shifted from one place to another. In one city a shekel or cubit could mean one thing. In another city it meant something else entirely. In one marketplace, barley was measured by the handful. Whose hand? In one place distance was measured by a bow shot or a day's travel. Which archer? Whose legs?

By the time of the New Testament, everything in life was more standardized because more of the world was under one rule. A money system was in place and there were government-established standards for weights and measurements. (Yes, the government was already stepping in with its standards. No FDA yet, though.)

Money

As you read the Bible, some terms you will find for money include the
terms below. You'll notice that some equal weights rather than currency.
That is because scales were used in the marketplace. These weights or coins
were put on one side of the scales and the merchandise was put on the
other side. That would make for a heavy change purse, wouldn't it?

Bible term		Approximate modern equivalent
Farthing		¼ cent
Quadrans		¼ cent
Mite		⅛ cent
Denarius	a day's wage	1 penny
Didrachma	½ Jewish shekel	32 cents
Drachma		16 cents
Shekel (royal)		0.5 ounce
Shekel (common)		0.4 ounce
Shekel (temple)	½ or ⅓ shekel	0.2 ounce
Talent (light)	3,000 shekels	66 pounds
Talent	125 libra	88 pounds
Mina	50 shekels	1.6 pounds

Weights and Measures

Liquids, like wine or oil, were measured in rectangular containers shaped a
little like a bathtub. They were called baths and came in different sizes.
Solids, like cereals and grains, were measured in tublike containers of different sizes. The largest was an ephah and was big enough to hold a small
adult. Another way to measure was with scales. Premeasured weights were
placed on one side of the scales and the merchandise was placed on the
other side priced according to weight.

Here are some weights and measurements that you might see as you read
the Bible. Keep in mind, though, that in the Old Testament they were less
standardized.

Bible term		*Approximate modern equivalent*
Liquid Measures		
Log		0.5 pint
Hin	⅙ bath	6 pints
Bath	liquid measurement	38.5 pints
Cor	homer	48.5 gallons
Homer	10 baths	90 gallons
Dry Measure		
Kab		3.5 pints
Omer	⅒ ephah	38.5 pints
Ephah		⅕ bushel
Distances		
Finger span		¾ inch
Palm		3 inches
Span	½ cubit	9 inches
Cubit		17.5 inches
Pace		1 yard
Fathom		6 feet
Reed	6 cubits	8 feet
Furlong		202 yards

3. Where Did the Bible Come From?

Who wrote it?

Who compiled it?

How did it get to us in the form that it's in?

HOW THE BIBLE CAME TO BE

So, How Was the Bible Actually Written?

We know the Bible now in rearview. We can look back from our viewpoint through history and see how it all came to be. But in order to really understand the Bible, we have to be able to look from the perspective of the writers, as they were experiencing life.

The people whose writings make up our Bible didn't know that their work would one day be collected into the Holy Scriptures. They weren't thinking they were going to be on a best-seller list. They were like we are: driven by the problems they were trying to solve and the ideologies that they felt passionately about.

- Moses wrote because he didn't want the history of God's provision to be forgotten. He wrote in the style in which he felt comfortable—narrative. He just told the facts as they happened, or as God told him they happened. He is the only person we know of who actually took dictation from God, at least when he wrote down the Ten Commandments.
- David didn't set out to write psalms that could be translated into praise music today. He just wrote about the parts of life that he was processing (even the less than shiny ones) and they became a part of Psalms.
- Jeremiah didn't make a plan to write a book that would fall three books after Ecclesiastes in the Bible. Jeremiah's heart was broken because his people continued, over and over, to fall away from God. Jeremiah knew that this would lead to their own destruction. So when God called Jeremiah to be a prophet, Jeremiah pulled out all the stops to convince them to turn back. He used metaphors. He used dramatic language. He forecast the consequences of their behavior. His style of writing poured out of who he was and how he communicated.

Each person who wrote a part of the Bible wrote from his specific place and time in history. What made their writing unique was that God breathed His truth through them. He used them exactly where they were, but guided them to record exactly what He needed. Today we think of this kind of thing as dictation, but that's not how it worked (except the one time with Moses). God didn't speak the words and let the writers take shorthand. It was more miraculous than that. He breathed His words into their lives so that when they wrote from their hearts, God was in it.

So, Who Decided What Books to Include in the Old Testament?

By the time civilization was grown up enough to keep historical records, the Old Testament was already collected into pretty much the same books that we have in our Old Testament today. The books were considered sacred because of their history and because of the power that evidenced itself when they were read. The first five books (called the Books of the Law, or the Torah, or the Pentateuch) were the basis of the Hebrew faith. The books of the prophets were studied and quoted in Hebrew worship. Each book had proven itself over and over again. Eventually this collection was called the Old Testament.

Remember that as the Old Testament was being written, the world was rather new and in the process of organizing itself. Languages and nationalities were being born. Technology was being birthed and then advancing. We humans were figuring out how to keep track of ourselves. In the midst of all that, the early theologians (which usually meant wise men who worked in the temple or synagogues) were discussing and rediscussing the power of the Bible, which at that time was called something like the "Law

DID YOU KNOW?

One of the big tests for the authority of Old Testament books was the test of the writer. The first five books (Genesis, Exodus, Leviticus, Numbers, Deuteronomy) were believed to be written by Moses. The rest were believed to be written by prophets (people to whom God manifested His truth). Some of the later books that don't appear in our Bible, but appear in others, were discounted because their authors were closer to historians than prophets.

and the Prophets." They were also discussing what their responsibility was in caring for the manuscripts and in passing them down through the generations. There were task forces formed (called councils) to specifically discuss and decide about these kinds of things.

In the final roll call, there were several different organizations of the Old Testament. Some versions kept 1 & 2 Kings as one book. Others made them two books. Some included some books written after 400 B.C. (called the Apocrypha, described above), but others didn't. The thirty-nine books listed on page 14 as the Old Testament were present in all of the versions, though they were organized in a variety of ways.

So, Who Decided What Books to Include in the New Testament?

By the time the New Testament was "canonized" (officially recognized as a complete collection of books), a very important discovery had been made among church leadership: the committee. While there had been a task force or two involved in recognizing the Old Testament canon, the early church had plenty of committee meetings about what books really were inspired by God and were to be included in what we call the New Testament.

By the late fourth century, the same twenty-seven books that you find in your New Testament were considered the finished New Testament. Even though committees or councils met, however, the canon of the New Testament wasn't something that arbitrary groups of people decided. These people merely recognized what books were standing the tests of authorship and authority. The books stood for themselves. It's just that by that time, humanity was organized enough to recognize it in a corporate kind of way.

If you want more details, grab a Bible dictionary or encyclopedia and look up "canonicity." You'll find a lot of information about what scrolls were found where and what historians mentioned what books. You can be sure that there has been no shortage of cross-referencing and cataloguing or research. What we often treat as casual and everyday was taken seriously in the time when the New Testament and Old Testament were being recognized as finished and complete.

Chapters and Verses

DID YOU KNOW?

Today when you open most Bibles you will find the books of the Bible divided into chapters and verses. This is not the way the Bible was originally written. Originally the books in the Bible were just writings. They were letters. They were sermons. They were stories. Except for the Psalms, which were numbered as songs, the other books were written in the form of letters, sermons, and stories.

By the fifth century, in some manuscripts the Gospels were divided into chapterlike divisions. Then in the Middle Ages a variety of systems were used to mark off texts that could be used for public worship. It wasn't until the thirteenth century, though, that Stephen Langton (chancellor of the University of Paris) divided the Vulgate (a widely used Latin translation) into chapters. Then around 1551 Robert Estienne (a printer in Paris) divided Langton's chapters into verses. These divisions became standard and have been used ever since.

Can you imagine how much harder it would have been to find John 3:16, or any other verse, without the 3:16?

WHERE'D WE GET THE TRANSLATIONS?

Making copies of the Bible, before printing presses, was a HUGE deal. Men, called scribes, dedicated their whole lives to the tedious task of copying the manuscripts l-e-t-t-e-r by l-e-t-t-e-r, line by line. Translating the Bible from its original language into another language was an even HUGER deal. It meant that mere people were going to make choices about what God was actually saying.

The Old Testament was originally written in Aramaic and Hebrew (two closely related languages). This makes sense when you know that all of its writers were Hebrews. The New Testament was originally written in Greek because that was the common language of that day (Alexander the Great had conquered the whole area by then and the standard language was Greek).

The first translation that we know of was when the Hebrew Old Testament was translated into Greek. It was called the Septuagint (sep-TU-a-jint).

It was called that because the translation was completed by seventy-two men, six from each of the twelve tribes of Israel. (Remember "sep" often means seven. A "septuagenarian" is a seventy-year-old.)

Since the Septuagint, there have been many translations. Maybe the most famous is the King James Bible, famous for its old English thee's and thou's. Other translations you might have heard of are the New International Version, the Revised Standard Version, and the New American Standard Bible.

People often talk about Bible translations in the same tone of voice in which they talk about politics or religion. In other words, they don't take it lightly. In fact, they can come to blows disagreeing about it. On one hand, it's a good thing that we take seriously the way we treat God's Word. On the other hand, the purpose of the Bible is to teach us to live lives that please God. We honor God's Word the most when we obey it, not when we defend a particular version of it.

There are two main schools of thought about translating.

- **Word-for-Word:** Each individual word is translated into its equivalent in the new language. These translations can be a little tougher to read and sometimes a little awkward. Some languages use articles and prepositions differently than others. Sometimes there is not an equivalent word. Sometimes you end up with more technical-sounding words in an effort to be exact, so overall the translation is harder to read.

- **Thought-for-Thought:** Rather than translating each word one at a time, the translator looks at the whole phrase or sentence and asks: "How can I translate this thought into a phrase that means the same thing?" Because of this, these versions are often easier to read.

Which method is better? They both have their place. *Word-for-word* translations (like the King James Version or the New American Standard) are great for doing in-depth studies of a single verse or word. But a *thought-for-thought* translation (like the New International Version or the New Living Translation) is great for daily reading and understanding. You might hear word-for-word translations called "study translations" and thought-for-thought translations called "reading translations." It wouldn't be a bad idea to have one of each on your bookshelf.

Here is how the most popular versions of the English Bible fit on the spectrum:

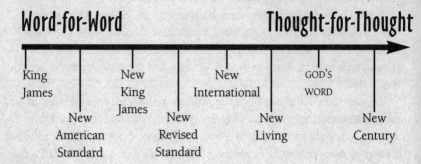

Would You Like Study Helps with Your Bible?

These days you can buy a Bible with as many options as a new car. You can buy a plain Bible, or you can buy a Bible with lots of extra stuff to help you understand and apply the information inside. You can buy a leather-bound Bible to last a lifetime or a paper-bound Bible to hopefully last through Middle School camp. You can buy a Bible with colorful maps and a concordance in the back for those times you want to look up a verse or a specific word. You can buy a Bible with lists in the back so you can find verses that will apply to your specific situation. All of these features help you better understand and navigate your Bible.

There are other features you can choose from, too. *Study Bibles* give you background, historical data, and explanations of hard-to-understand verses. *Devotional Bibles* often give you a devotional plan for reading the Bible each day. They give you a daily Bible passage to read and give you a devotional thought (kind of like a short sermon) on the passage.

If you are motivated to read and understand the Bible, you'll want to find a Bible that works for you. If it looks too complicated for your purposes, look around some more. Ask people that you know and respect who read the Bible what they like about their translation. Ask the clerks in the store what they know about the translations on their shelves. As long as you are using trustworthy translations, find the Bible that will be most inviting to you to spend time reading it. If you aren't reading it, you won't benefit from its power to change your life.

Which Translation?

You'll note some initials after most Bible references that are listed in a book. If you don't see any initials, look on the copyright page of the book and you'll probably see that one specific translation is used or that one is used unless otherwise noted. In this book, if there are no initials, the translation is the NIV or New International Version. Here are some typical translation abbreviations you may see.

GW	God's Word
KJV	King James Version
NASB	New American Standard Bible
NCV	New Century Version
NIV	New International Version
NKJV	New King James Version
NLT	New Living Translation
NRSV	New Revised Standard Version
TLB	The Living Bible
TM	The Message

4. The Basic Anatomy of the Bible

A roadmap for your journey. . .

THE BASIC INFO

T he Bible is the story of God's reaching out to His creation, to people, to us. It opens with the creation of the earth and closes with the end of life as we know it. There are two main sections of the Bible. The first is the Old Testament, written before Christ came to earth. The second is the New Testament, written after Christ's birth, life, death, resurrection, and return to heaven.

Old Testament

The Old Testament is made up of thirty-nine different "books." These books were inspired by God (see "How the Bible Came to Be") but written by different people in many walks of life and for many different purposes.

Some of the books are just one step beyond oral tradition. They are stories to be passed down to generations to come. Some of the books are almost legal documents; they are the rules and regulations of the day. Some are poetry, songs, hymns, proverbs. Some are sermons and prophecies.

The writers wrote out of their own abilities and context. It wasn't like they were saying to themselves, "I'm going to write a book and JUST MAYBE it will be included in the Bible one day." No. They wrote because an issue needed to be addressed or some history needed to be recorded. They responded to that need in the most effective way they could think of. God wrote the Bible through these writers as they responded to life around them.

Even though the Old Testament didn't speak about Jesus in the same biographical way that the New Testament did, the focus of the Old Testament is on God's solution to humanity's problem: the future coming of Christ. In the Old Testament Jesus is referred to as the promised one, Messiah, Immanuel, the redeemer. God's promise to Abraham included a promise that Jesus would come through Abraham's bloodline, the Jewish people. This is why the history of the Jewish people was so important: Jesus was climbing down that family tree. This is the significance of all the sacrifices you read about in the Old Testament: Jesus was promised as the ultimate sacrifice for sin.

New Testament

The second section of the Bible includes twenty-seven different documents or books. All of these books were written in the first hundred years after Jesus lived. Like the Old Testament, they were written by different people in different circumstances and for different reasons, but inspired by God. These documents were all pulled together and recognized as the collection we call the New Testament.

The New Testament is made of books that tell the story of Jesus' life, death, and resurrection; the story of the church; and letters written to encourage and instruct those churches.

OLD TESTAMENT ORGANIZATION

Typically the Old Testament is broken down into these categories:

The Law

Written by Moses himself, these books tell about the beginning of the world and the Jewish nation. They tell history through stories. They also give guidelines for life and worship. They are a mixture of narratives and instruction.

These books (also called the Torah or Pentateuch) are the basis for the Hebrew faith.

- Genesis
- Exodus
- Leviticus
- Numbers
- Deuteronomy

The History Books

These books tell true stories of historical events. They span the time from when the Hebrews reentered Israel after leaving Egypt, through the divided kingdom and the exile into Babylon and Assyria, and then until the Hebrews reentered Jerusalem after the exile. (Theirs is a rocky past.)

- Joshua
- 1 & 2 Samuel
- Ezra

- Judges
- 1 & 2 Kings
- Nehemiah

- Ruth
- 1 & 2 Chronicles
- Esther

The Wisdom Books

These books are more experiential. Some are stories, but they are not from an informational point of view as much as a grappling-with-life point of view. Jesus would have called the books The Writings. Others have called them "wisdom literature."

- Job
- Proverbs
- Song of Solomon

- Psalms
- Ecclesiastes

Prophetic Books

The prophets were the philosophers of the day, the street preachers, the Billy Grahams of the ancient Hebrew world. They told it like it was. In the process, through God's guidance, they also sometimes told it the way it would be when Christ came hundreds of years later. Even if they did do a little future-telling, they were not like fortune-tellers or psychics. They talked about the future for the purpose of their people having hope and living clean lives within that hope. The prophetic books are divided into two categories. The first five books are books by the "major" prophets. It's not so much because they were greater than the others, but their writings are longer and we do know more about them.

- Isaiah
- Lamentations
- Daniel

- Jeremiah
- Ezekiel

The rest of the books are by prophets considered "minor" prophets. The lives of the prophets below were more obscure and their writings are shorter.

- Hosea
- Jonah
- Zephaniah

- Joel
- Micah
- Haggai

- Amos
- Nahum
- Zechariah

- Obadiah
- Habakkuk
- Malachi

NEW TESTAMENT ORGANIZATION

The New Testament is typically thought of being divided into these categories:

The Gospels

These are similar to biographies of the life of Jesus Christ, though some writers organized events in different order.

- Matthew

- Mark

- Luke

- John

IN CONTEXT

The prophecies of the Old Testament do not appear in the Bible in the order that the prophets lived or worked. (If anything they are roughly in order by length from the longest to the shortest.) So when you read through their messages, keep in mind that they are not chronological. But they all preached to Israel or Judah between the time that the Hebrews resettled the land, through their exile into foreign lands, and eventual return home. These writings were the spiritual guides of that time.

History

There is only one history book in the New Testament besides the Gospels. It's really a sequel to the Gospel written by Luke. It is the story of the beginning of the New Testament church and the spread of the good news of Christ.

- Acts

Letters or Epistles [uh-PIS-uhls]

We know the first thirteen letters were written by the apostle Paul. The last three of those letters are called his pastoral letters because they were written to pastors rather than whole churches. The letters after the letter to the Hebrews are called general epistles because they weren't written to any one specific person or church.

- Romans
- 1 & 2 Corinthians
- Galatians
- Ephesians
- Philippians
- Colossians
- 1 & 2 Thessalonians
- 1 & 2 Timothy
- Titus
- Philemon
- Hebrews
- James
- 1 & 2 Peter
- 1, 2, & 3 John
- Jude

Prophecy

There is only one book of prophecy in the New Testament. This book is about the "end times" or the "second coming" (meaning, of Jesus). It could also be called apocalyptic (meaning, end of the world).

- Revelation

WRITING STYLES

Because the Bible was written by so many different authors facing so many different slices of life, it is written in a lot of different literary styles. We read each book best when we understand the perspective of the author. Here are some categories that might help.

Historical Narratives

Genesis, Exodus, Judges, and the Acts are some prime examples of historical narratives. They teach us about history but not just the facts of history. They tell us the story of history, the people, the places, the marriages, the family conflicts. Historical narratives were one step above oral tradition. They were the way history was passed down. The author wanted to describe events and to tell about heroes and villains.

Wisdom Writings

Often these books are called poetic, but not the "Roses are red, Violets are blue" type of poetry. Hebrew poetry wasn't so concerned with rhyming as it was with symmetry and profound thoughts. It was called poetry because of its structure and style. Psalms, Proverbs, Ecclesiastes, and Song of Solomon are classic poetry books, perhaps even poetic philosophy books that cut a slice of life and place it on a plate with presentation as a primary concern. Wisdom writings are to be experienced, savored, rolled around in your mind, and digested bit by bit. They are life's encounters recorded through one writer's perspective and applied as it was meaningful for him.

Prophecies

A bulk of the Old Testament is made up of prophetic passages. Isaiah through Malachi (the last book) are prophetic books. These prophets spoke to their own culture, as well as to the future. When they were writing, the only Bible to speak of was the Book of the Law (the first five books of the

Old Testament). Today when we think of hearing God speak or of His revealing Himself, we think of the wealth of His words we have in the Bible. Back then, though, they were still waiting for fresh news from God. They got it through the prophets. The prophets were the guys who simply could not sit still watching their people decay spiritually.

Teaching Passages

There are many passages that are specifically meant to teach us. They aren't giving us a story and letting us draw our conclusions. They aren't poetry or narratives. They are lay-it-on-the-table, this-is-how-it-is-and-will-be truth. They are intended to train us and to teach us, to inform us and to form us. The Gospels are filled with teaching passages from Jesus. Much of the epistles or letters in the New Testament include them as well.

Parables

The Gospels include many of Jesus' parables. The importance of these passages was not the facts of the story. The importance was the principles underneath the story line. When we read the story of the woman who continues to knock on someone's door until he answers, it's not important what the woman wanted or whether a woman would have knocked on a door that long. What is important is that when we keep seeking answers from God, we have a better chance of finding them the longer we persevere.

Epistles or Letters

Much of the New Testament is written in the form of letters, personal letters to churches and to people. They include personal information at the beginning and the end. It's like reading someone else's e-mail. You understand it best when you know what questions the writer was answering. So the more we know about the churches that received the mail, the better we understand the letter.

HAVE YOU THOUGHT ABOUT IT THIS WAY?

Cable Station Synopsis

It might be easier to understand the whole writing-in-style thing if you think about cable TV stations. TV is going the way of radio these days in that each station is finding a niche or format and fitting its shows within that format. Except for the traditional networks, the cooking shows are on a channel about cooking. The sports shows are on a channel about sports. If books of the Bible were assigned to cable channels, they might divide up like this.

Television for Women

Esther, Ruth, and Song of Solomon: These would definitely fit in with "chick" TV. Women's stories, problems, issues, and interests.

Science Fiction or Psychic Channel

The writings of the prophets of the Old Testament and the Book of Revelation would definitely fit into this kind of genre, even though there is nothing fictional or fake about them. No per-minute charges, either, on their hotlines. But amazing visions and a future like you wouldn't (but can) believe.

Real Life TV

Joshua, Judges, 1 & 2 Samuel, 1 & 2 Kings. Talk about action, suspense, and adventure. If they had a cameraman running behind, we'd be watching them whether they fuzzed out the Philistine faces or not.

Advice TV

Proverbs: everyday wisdom to make decisions by—without the fights, the weird clothes, or the tearful confrontations.

History Channel or even the News

Genesis, Exodus, 1 & 2 Chronicles, and Acts: These books would be prime targets for who, what, when, where. They recorded not only what happened, but often what impact it had on the culture.

Music Station

Music video programming has never seen the likes of the lyrics in the Psalms. Just what kind of spin would you put on Psalm 18? Talk about special effects.

Biography Channel

Ezra, Nehemiah, Job, and the Gospels: All these books give the story of one man's life.

Christian TV

The epistles or letters of the New Testament could be the meat and potatoes of Christian TV stations. These were letters written specifically to Christians dealing with real issues. Put a host writer in front of a microphone and let him go.

THE WHOLE BIBLE IN ONE-LINERS

The whole next section is dedicated to the content of the Bible, book by book. Before you take on that mass of information, though, here is the whole Bible in one-liners.

Old Testament:

Genesis:	God created the world, gave us the choice to love Him, and began His plan to restore us through a good man named Abraham.
Exodus:	In Egypt, Abraham's descendants grew into the Hebrew nation, then they headed back home.
Leviticus:	God gives the Hebrews guidelines for worship and sanitation to survive their journey.
Numbers:	Because of their lack of faith, the Hebrews take a forty-year detour through the desert.
Deuteronomy:	Moses says good-bye, gives a history lesson, and gives some guidelines for loving and worshiping God.
Joshua:	The Hebrews resettled their land, after over four hundred years away, by facing down the squatters in every city.
Judges:	The Hebrews organize into a nation back in their homeland and are led by wise judges.

Ruth: One family's story about God's provision.

1 & 2 Samuel: Samuel leads Israel, then he anoints King Saul. After Saul, King David rules and his family suffers.

1 & 2 Kings: Solomon ruled Israel, then the kingdom divided in two. Finally the Hebrews are exiled to foreign lands.

1 & 2 Chronicles: Israel's story from David's reign until the exile into Babylon, but from a spiritual (not political) perspective.

Ezra: The Hebrews returned from Babylon (where they were in exile) and rebuilt the temple.

Nehemiah: More Hebrews returned from Babylon and rebuilt Jerusalem's wall.

Esther: The Hebrews survived exile in Persia because of a Jewish royal beauty contest winner.

Job: Bad times don't change the nature of God.

Psalms: Lyric sheets from Old Testament temple worship. Songs about facing life and worshiping God.

Proverbs: Nuggets of wisdom for dealing with everyday life.

Ecclesiastes: I had it all, and it didn't mean anything without God. Sincerely, King Solomon.

Song of Songs: I'm passionately in love, and I can't stop thinking about her! By Solomon.

Isaiah: Pay attention. God has a master plan in the works and we need to be a part of it.

Jeremiah: Prepare to face the consequences of living apart from God. Know that God's plan is still in place.

Lamentations: What we dreaded has happened. Our sin has destroyed us. My heart is broken.

Ezekiel: Here are some visions I saw from God's perspective on how we've lived our lives and of heaven.

Daniel:	Here are the stories of Daniel, a Jewish exile in Persia, and his visions of the future.
Hosea:	Ephraim, you are as unfaithful to God as a prostitute to her husband. Turn around!
Joel:	Because of our sin, it's going to get worse before it gets better. But it will get better one day.
Amos:	By human standards, you're looking okay, but by God's standards, you're failing.
Obadiah:	Attention, people of Edom: You've bullied Israel and now you'll answer to God Himself.
Jonah:	Jonah unwillingly prophesied to a wicked place and was disappointed at the good turnout.
Micah:	We are immoral and headed for destruction. Only God can deliver us from ourselves.
Nahum:	No matter how strong evil seems, God will do away with it when He is ready.
Habakkuk:	God, why don't you stop bad things from happening?
Zephaniah:	God will hold us accountable for our actions. All of them.
Haggai:	Don't ignore what matters most—your relationship with your God and creator!
Zechariah:	Finish the temple and get your relationship with God in working order. The Messiah is coming!
Malachi:	Worshiping God is not about doing the least to get by. Be wholehearted instead.

New Testament

| Matthew: | Dear Hebrews, Jesus is the Messiah that God promised through the prophets and here's how I know. |

Mark: Hey Romans, Jesus was a servant-king. Look what He did!

Luke: Amazing news! Jesus is God and yet totally human. He understands our journey.

John: It really is true. Jesus Christ is God Himself.

Acts: A new church organizes: Jesus' sacrifice makes us right with God. Spread the news!

Romans: Dear church, The only way we can be right with God is through faith.

1 Corinthians: Dear church, Don't be like the world around you. Be who God made you to be, pure and effective.

2 Corinthians: Dear church, Here's who I am. Now let me tell you who you should be.

Galatians: Dear church, You can't earn God's approval by obeying rules. It takes faith.

Ephesians: Dear church, Receive God's amazing love for you. Then, love each other well.

Philippians: Dear church, Knowing you brings joy to me. Knowing God brings joy to all of us.

Colossians: Dear church, Faith in Christ is enough. Don't add anything else to it.

1 Thessalonians: Dear church, Look forward to Christ's return!

2 Thessalonians: Dear church, Look forward to Christ's return, but keep living full lives and working hard!

1 Timothy: Dear Tim, You're doing well. Here are some things to remember about leading a church.

2 Timothy: Dear Tim, Come soon. I don't know how much longer I'll be here. Keep the faith!

Titus: Dear Titus, Here are some helpful hints about leading your church.

Philemon: Dear Philemon, Forgive Onesimus not as a run-
              away, but as your brother in faith.

Hebrews: To all Jewish Christians: Now that Christ has
              come, focus on Him rather than the rituals that
              pointed you to Him.

James: Yes, salvation is by faith, but faith without action
              is useless.

1 & 2 Peter: These are difficult times. Let your faith help you
              endure. Don't let go just because troubles come.

1 John: Ignore false teaching. Live righteously. Love each
              other. Know that Jesus was God in the flesh.

2 John: Keep your chin up and your hearts open, but
              keep a close watch on your faith.

3 John: Keep up the good work! I'll be there soon to deal
              with the power struggle.

Jude: Watch out for people who use God's grace as an
              excuse for irresponsibility!

Revelation: Here's the last page of world history—the end of
              the world as we know it.

5. What Does the Bible Say?

The best way to know what the Bible says is to read it. The next best way is to look at the book-by-book summaries here.

WHAT DOES THE BIBLE SAY?

That's a big question. The following sections are a medium-sized answer divided into a book-by-book summary. Each book is categorized for you so that you'll know upfront what kind of situation the writer was facing and what kind of

SCRIPTURE BITS

Before you read about what the Bible says, read what the Bible says about itself:

For the word of God is full of living power. It is sharper than the sharpest knife, cutting deep into our innermost thoughts and desires. It exposes us for what we really are.

Hebrews 4:12 NLT

All Scripture is inspired by God and is useful to teach us what is true and to make us realize what is wrong in our lives. It straightens us out and teaches us to do what is right. It is God's way of preparing us in every way, fully equipped for every good thing God wants us to do.

2 Timothy 3:16–17 NLT

And remember, it is a message to obey, not just to listen to. If you don't obey, you are only fooling yourself. For if you just listen and don't obey, it is like looking at your face in a mirror but doing nothing to improve your appearance. You see yourself, walk away, and forget what you look like. But if you keep looking steadily into God's perfect law—the law that sets you free—and if you do what it says and don't forget what you heard, then God will bless you for doing it.

James 1:22–25 NLT

information he was giving. Each book is a slice of life laid out on a platter. It's a little piece of somebody's life that God spoke through.

Just a little note: You'll find throughout the Old Testament that God taught people a lot through object lessons. The feasts that the Jews instituted and celebrated were reminders of significant events in their history. God asked them to build memorials from time to time. The prophets often used objects or actions to teach. It's a pretty cool thing to realize that God works with people in practical ways. He did the same thing when He embodied Himself in the New Testament. He taught in parables, everyday stories, down-to-earth examples. It makes you wonder, doesn't it, where we ever got the idea that God was a distant deity who doesn't dig into our lives. If the Bible reveals anything, it's that God meets us right where we are and teaches us in every possible way that we'll understand.

OLD TESTAMENT BOOK SUMMARIES

The following pages include a little information about each of the books in the Old Testament. They are marked off in sections (law, history, poetry, prophecy). The books are in the order that they appear in the Bible.

For each book you can read some stats and a one-line overview, or you can dig a little deeper and read over the major stories or points of that book.

As with anything else in this world, there are a lot of differing opinions about a lot of the details listed here. Sometimes there are different guesses about who the author was or if he was the only author. For our purposes you'll see the most generally accepted facts listed.

For instance, there might have possibly been other writers included in the Psalms, but we've told you the ones we're sure of. In the back of this book is a list of sources that you can use to explore all the possible scenarios for these details.

THE LAW

The first five books of the Bible are called the Law of Moses, or the Books of the Law (also the Torah or Pentateuch). In the New Testament, when Jesus is quoted talking about the "law and the prophets," the "law" refers to these first five books. Moses is credited with writing all five of these books.

These first five books lay the groundwork for a lot of life. They were the survival manuals for the Jewish nation, the descendants of Abraham, the recipients of the covenant he established with God. It is in these five books that we learn the stories of the beginning of the world itself, as well as the beginnings of the different cultures and languages of the world. It's in these books that the Hebrews learned how to survive as nomadic people in their desert wanderings (from how to deal with mold to what to do about PMS). It's in these books that the Hebrews learned to build their first church and how to maintain it. It's in these books that the priesthood was established as well as the kosher diet and the first pyramid personnel management system. It's in these books that a people began their journey of knowing God and living in peace with Him.

HAVE YOU THOUGHT ABOUT IT THIS WAY?

The stories in these books aren't necessarily G-rated even though we teach them in simple form in children's Sunday school. They are set in a primal, violent time in world history. God worked through these people as they were. He didn't pretty them up before He told us about them.

CONTEXT

The Law of the Old Testament
- Genesis
- Exodus
- Leviticus
- Numbers
- Deuteronomy

GENESIS

IN CONTEXT

Here's the scoop. . .

Written: *around 1450 B.C.*

Written by: *Moses*

Writing style: *historical accounts of true stories*

One-liner: *God created the world, reached out to people, and gave them the choice to reach back.*

The Lay of the Land

The Book of Genesis covers a lot of historical ground. The places, the people, and the events that you'll read about through the rest of the Bible all find their roots in Genesis.

It is in this book that God established the world and His relationship with the people of that world, first through Adam and Eve, then Noah, then Abraham and his descendants.

Creation

Genesis describes the creation of the world in very concrete terms. God spoke us and our surroundings into being. The world was ideal when God made it. The first people were placed in a paradise called the Garden of Eden and asked to tend that garden, to build a friendship with God, and to obey Him. You probably know how that story goes. The dad was Adam, the mom was Eve. . . .

The First Dysfunctional Family

Adam and Eve were the first and only earth-dwellers to experience the world as innocent ADULTS. They woke up for the first time able to walk and run and love and enjoy God's creation. Before long they did the one thing God asked them not to do, and innocent adulthood was gone forever. They left the ideal garden and the kind of life we know began: sweat, labor, pain, and disappointment. They lost their first two sons to violent, fatal sibling rivalry. It was not a happy time. But Adam and Eve did what we do today. They picked themselves up and dusted themselves off, and with the forgiveness and guidance of Almighty God, they started all over again. Their world was changed forever, but their God was still the same.

Noah

The descendants of the first family disregarded God more and more. The world became a mess. (Perhaps more of a mess than it is now.) It was such a mess that God thought about scrapping the project all together (Genesis 6:5–8). There was one man, though, who remained faithful. God preserved that man's family: Noah, his wife, and their three married sons.

God preserved Noah by asking for his obedience. God told Noah to build a very big boat. There is a good chance that until this point it hadn't even rained in the world yet, so building a boat was a wild thing for Noah to do. Then came all the animals; then came the floods. Everything on the earth was destroyed except the creatures on that boat.

When it was all over, Noah recommitted himself, his family, and this freshly laundered world to follow the Creator once again. We are all descendants of Noah's family.

Abraham

One of Noah's descendants (more than a few generations down) was Abraham (at one point he was known as Abram). God established a special relationship with Abraham. He promised that Abraham would be the father of a great nation. At the time of this promise, Abraham was very old and had never had children! God also asked Abraham to pick up and move to a new place, Canaan. Canaan was the place that we know as Israel today.

Eventually Abraham and his also-old wife, Sarah, did have a child, Isaac, way past their childbearing years. Today, Abraham and Sarah would have had top-selling autobiographies as well as incredible tabloid marketability. But in their day and time, they were just two people who (after some laughter and "are you sure's?") believed God would do what He said.

If you've hung around kids' programs at church much, you may have heard the motion song, "Father Abraham Had Many Sons." The song can go on forever. Abraham's descendants did, too. All from two little old people who believed God could do the impossible.

You may have also heard of Sodom and Gomorrah, some pretty wicked cities. Abraham's nephew, Lot, lived in one of these cities. Abraham saved Lot from destruction just before God burned the towns to the ground. It was Lot's wife who looked back at her home and died immediately, transformed into salt.

The Israelites

Genesis is really about a family tree. First it's about the family tree of the whole world. Then it's about Abraham's family tree. This is why you'll find genealogies galore. (As irritating as it may be to women today, most of this was defined according to the dads. That's an ironic twist, considering that the test of whether a person is Jewish depends on the nationality of Mom more than Dad.)

Abraham's son, Isaac, had twin sons, Esau and Jacob. In an amazing turn of events (not to mention deceit and disguise), Jacob, the younger of the twins, got the birthright. Because of that, he became the leader of the family. God changed Jacob's name to Israel (names meant a lot more back then than they do now and there wasn't any paperwork to fill out). Thus Jacob, or Israel, became the head of the family and his descendants were called the Israelites (or Israelis or Hebrews or Jewish as we know them today). The land they settled in was also called Israel.

Jacob had twelve sons and one daughter. His sons became the patriarchs (or head honchos) of their families, called tribes. (You'll sometimes hear them described as the twelve tribes of Israel.) It was a Middle Eastern *Bonanza* in the making.

Joseph

Jacob's (Israel's) favorite sons were his two youngest, Joseph and Benjamin. They were the sons of Jacob's favorite wife, Rachel. (He had two wives, Leah and Rachel, who were sisters. Now *that's* a wild story on its own. Genesis 29)

Joseph was the confident sort and his older brothers resented his dreams and aspirations, whether they came from God or not. (Remember this was a barbaric time.) Joseph's brothers resorted to violence in their rage at their cocky younger brother. While they were in the wilderness together, they beat Joseph and almost decided to kill him. Instead they settled for selling him into slavery.

This slavery eventually led Joseph to Egypt. He started out in poverty, but despite false accusations and jail time, with some dream interpreting on the side, Joseph became one of the king's most trusted men.

Talk about a twist of fate. Later, when Jacob's land was filled with a fierce famine, he sent his sons to Egypt begging for food. Who do you think was the man in charge of giving out portions? None other than their long-lost brother Joseph. You can imagine the shuffling feet and wary glances. It was a younger sibling's opportunity for revenge.

But in the end, Joseph knew that his brothers' foolish and violent actions had, in the long run, set the stage for his family's survival in the famine. Eventually the whole family moved to Egypt and established a long-term residence there.

AN EXPLANATION YOU MIGHT NEED

DID YOU KNOW?

The historical period Genesis describes is a time in which polygamy (having more than one wife at a time) was accepted. Since it was a culture in which men held the power, there were multiple wives more than multiple husbands. Not only were there wives, there were also concubines (sexual partners, but not marriage partners, that made up a harem). This is difficult to reconcile in today's world, where polygamy exists but is not considered a standard way of living and is often against the law. While polygamy was accepted, throughout history God honored monogamous husband/wife relationships (after all, He didn't created Adam and Eve and Isabel).

There were also several occasions listed in Genesis where a woman offered her servant or maid to her husband to father his children. Sarah tried it with Abraham and brought grief in her family that continues until this day. Leah and Rachel both adopted this practice with their servants. It was so important in that culture to have sons, as many of them as possible, that practices such as this were considered last resorts.

So, Where's God Going with All This?

Since the Bible, in its entirety, is really about Jesus, even this beginning book lays a foundation. When Adam and Eve disregarded God's one requirement for their paradise living, there was a snake involved. We believe this snake to be a force of evil (the devil, Lucifer, prince of darkness). When God explained the consequences of Eve's, Adam's, and the snake's actions, He said to the snake: "Because you have done this, cursed are you above all the livestock and all the wild animals! You will crawl on your belly and you will eat dust all the days of your life. And I will put enmity between you and the woman, and between your offspring and hers; he will crush your head, and you will strike his heel" (Genesis 3:14–15). This was probably a reference to Jesus' coming to conquer the powers of evil.

Also in God's promise to Abraham was the promise that the Messiah (the Savior, Jesus Christ) would come through that family line. As soon as people resorted to sin, God began His plan to restore us. So from Genesis 1, God, in the person of Jesus Christ, was the plan.

EXODUS

IN CONTEXT

Here's the scoop. . .

Written: *around 1450* B.C.

Written by: *Moses*

Writing style: *a chronological historical account*

One-liner: *In Egypt, Abraham's descendants grew into the Hebrew nation, then they headed back home.*

Post-Genesis

The Book of Exodus picks up the story line where the Book of Genesis ended. At the end of Genesis, the twelve sons of Israel (the man who had been named Jacob, remember) had come to live in Egypt. They did this because of a famine in their own land. They were able to do this because one brother, Joseph, had built his home and a great reputation in Egypt, so his brothers were welcome.

Once there, the family of Israel grew and grew. They became a small nation among the Egyptians and that was nerve-racking for the Egyptian king. What if they decided to overthrow the government? Because of his fears, he made the Israelites slaves. This began the first of many very dark times in Jewish history.

Even as slaves, the Hebrews (another name for the nation of Israel) continued to grow. (This had been promised by God to the very first ancestor of the Jewish nation, Abraham. Genesis 17) Pharaoh tried another form of population control: He let the female infants live but destroyed the male infants. In the midst of this tragedy, God raised up a leader named Moses, who would eventually stand up for his people and lead them to freedom.

Moses

Moses is the main character in Exodus (after God, that is).

Moses was born into a courageous family. When he was born, there was a decree from the king that all male babies should be destroyed. Moses' mom hid him for three months, then made a floating basket and hid him in the basket at the banks of the Nile River. His sister, Miriam, stood watch.

When the princess came to bathe in the river, she found the basket and adopted the bootleg Israelite baby. She gave him the name Moses (which means "out of the water"). Moses' sister, Miriam, showed quick wit and great timing. When the princess found baby Moses, Miriam immediately offered to go and find a Hebrew "baby-sitter." Of course Miriam brought back her own mom.

Moses grew up in the palace but as a young man was exiled from Egypt. (He killed an Egyptian for mistreating a Hebrew.) It was during this time of exile that God carved out Moses' life's mission: to free his people, to lead them back to Canaan, their promised land, and to establish the Ten Commandments on the way. Easy enough? You thought YOU had it rough....

Sure enough, Moses did lead the people out of Egypt and to the border of their homeland. It took him over forty years to do it and stress points galore, but he died a man who had stood at the edge of God's promise coming true.

The Passover

The Passover is one of the most significant rituals of the Jewish faith. It finds its origins in the last plague God sent to Egypt to convince the king to set the Hebrews free. During the plague, the angel of death swept through Egypt, taking the lives of the firstborn sons. The Hebrews were instructed to place the blood of a lamb on their doorposts. If they did so, their firstborn sons would be spared. There is a special meal associated with the Passover. Today we often call the celebration of that meal a "seder" (SAY-dur).

IN CONTEXT

Most of Exodus is about that journey to freedom, from Egypt, through the desert, to the Promised Land. The journey of the Israelites was a lot like the journey of modern believers: We leave the slavery of sin, we travel through an often difficult desert of a life, and then finally we get to our real home, heaven.

The Passover was a symbol of God's salvation through the blood of an innocent life. It was an accurate picture of Jesus Christ's sacrifice for the sins of His people. He was innocent, He was a firstborn, and He shed His blood. The last meal that Jesus shared with His disciples before His crucifixion was a Passover meal.

Stories from the Road

A lot of amazing things happened to the Israelites along their journey. Here are some favorites among the "remember whens."

The Red Sea. Just as the people left Egypt, the king changed his mind and sent his armies to bring them back. The people stood between chariots and spears and the Red Sea. God parted the waters so they could make their escape on dry ground. (Exodus 14:15–30)

Bread from Heaven. The people were in a desert for much of the trip. Each morning a breadlike substance would be lying on the ground like snow. This is how they ate. (Exodus 16:2–4)

The Quail. Once when the people were craving meat, quail came "out of nowhere" to supply a BBQ feast. (Exodus 16:13)

Water. Once it came from a rock (Exodus 17:2–6) and once a bitter stream turned sweet just for the Israelites' drinking. (Exodus 15:22–25)

Navigation. The people were led by a cloud by day and a pillar of fire by night. No need to ask directions when God is leading. (Exodus 13:21–22)

The Ten Commandments. God Himself wrote these on stone. Remember, this was before printing presses and electricity. Writing ten commands in stone was no little feat. (Exodus 20)

Moses' Glow. After Moses had spent time with God on the mountain, his face literally glowed. He had to wear a veil so the people could deal with him without being distracted. (Exodus 34:29–35)

LEVITICUS

IN CONTEXT

Here's the scoop. . .

Written: *around 1450 B.C.*

Written by: *Moses*

Writing style: *a book of guidelines*

One-liner: *God gives the Hebrews guidelines for worship and sanitation to survive their journey.*

A Holiness Instruction Manual

You can imagine that as a whole nation of people left Egypt to travel in the wilderness, there was a great need for organization. They were organized into tribes. They were also organized into roles: some were administrative assistants, others were ordained priests, etc. One family, the descendants of Levi, was assigned to be priests. They cared for the tabernacle (a portable temple). They helped with the sacrifices. They "kept house." They cared for the precious artifacts that reminded their people of the journey to freedom.

The Book of Leviticus is mostly a how-to manual for Israel's priests. It is a detailed instruction booklet for just about any situation that might arise. Keep in mind that the Israelites at this time could have been described as vagabonds: They lived in tents, and they moved often. Sanitation was a big concern. The priests were responsible for teaching the people what was "clean" and what was "unclean." There were guidelines regarding mildew, leprosy, disease, food, sin, sacrifices, and even holidays.

Holiness

The information found in Leviticus kept the people healthy and clean, but it also taught them something about God. It taught them that God is holy. The Bible doesn't actually say "cleanliness is next to godliness," but Leviticus does make a connection between God's holiness and our cleanliness. That connection probably saved the life of a wandering nation.

IN CONTEXT

Leviticus is a practical treatise on how to worship, how to live in community, and how to stay alive. Don't let the fancy-shmancy Latin-sounding name fool you. In the situation for which it was written, Leviticus is the most practical of books: sandal-meets-the-dirt-road kind of stuff.

Sacrifices

From the earliest historical records, animal sacrifices were a part of religious life. The concept of an innocent shedding its blood to atone for someone's bad deeds was a part of Jewish and Gentile history alike. (See Genesis 4:4–5.)

Leviticus gives specific guidelines for sacrifices: What animals? What kind? When? How? Sacrifices involved blood and a certain amount of brutality. They were a picture of the sacrifice that Jesus Christ eventually made for all of us; He in His innocence shedding His blood for our bad deeds. The sacrifices were an appalling demonstration of just how seriously God regards our sin.

NUMBERS

Here's the scoop. . .

Written: *around 1450 B.C.*

Written by: *Moses*

Writing style: *A mixture of stories and official logs or records*

One-liner: *Because of their lack of faith, the Hebrews take a forty-year detour through the desert.*

A Captain's Log

Numbers is a book of facts, figures, and events. It is a record, kept by Moses, of thirty-eight years of wandering.

Remember, the Hebrews had been delivered out of Egypt by God through miracle after miracle. (For instance, food that came like dew every morning and water that gushed out of rocks.) After two years of miracles and hardships, it looked like their journey was about to come to a wonderful end—then it happened.

The Israelites sent twelve spies into Israel to scope out just how big a task lay ahead in reclaiming the land. When the spies returned, ten of them were overwhelmed with fear. Only two of the spies, Joshua and Caleb, remembered what God had already brought them through and said, "We can do it with God's help."

After all God had done, the people doubted Him and were afraid to enter. Because of their lack of faith, God sent them back into the desert. There, they wandered for forty more years before trying again. In fact, everyone who was over twenty when they left Egypt died before entering Israel—except Joshua and Caleb.

Numbskull Awards

In many ways, Numbers is a book about failures: foolishness, acts of indiscretion, lack of judgment, poor choices, and just plain old sin. Here are the top five winners for foolish choices recorded in Numbers:

5. *Korah (Numbers 16)*. Korah got two buddies and 250 henchmen and staged an insurrection against Moses. Know what happened? The earth swallowed up Korah.

4. *The prophet Balaam (Numbers 22–24)*. Balaam was paid by King Balak (honorable mention in the Numbskull Awards) to put a curse on Israel. God interceded even to the point of making Balaam's own donkey try to reason with him. Can't get much worse than that.

3. *Miriam and Aaron (Numbers 12)*. Leave it to family. Moses' own sister and brother decided they wanted a bigger piece of the power. Instead, all Miriam got was a temporary case of leprosy and all they both got was a bigger piece of humble pie.

2. *The ten fearful spies (Numbers 13–14)*. These men were the leaders of their clans. They had witnessed God's provision. Yet, they turned chicken when they were within reach of what God had promised. They used their influence to destroy the faith of their people.

1. *The people (Numbers 11, 13–14)*. The all-time prize has to go to the Israelite people. Sure, it's not easy to trek through a desert, but God had been faithful. Out of 600,000 plus, all but two of them doubted God. They worshiped idols, they wished for captivity, they figuratively spit in God's face. These tactics didn't work well for them.

DEUTERONOMY

Here's the scoop. . .

Written: *around 1450 B.C.*

Written by: *Moses*

Writing style: *a mixture of stories and sermons*

One-liner: *Moses reminds the Hebrews of their history and gives them guidelines for loving and worshiping God.*

Famous Last Words

This book was written at a significant time. The Israelites had traveled for FORTY YEARS in the desert. They did this knowing that one day they would enter the land that had been promised to Abraham, their ancestor. When they had left Egypt (where they were slaves), there were 600,000+ people in the group over the age of twenty. By the time that Deuteronomy describes, just before they enter the land, only three of those people were still living (Moses, Joshua, and Caleb). A whole generation, the ones who had seen God's provision and heard His laws, had passed away. A new generation (or two) had arisen who only knew what they had heard second- or third-hand.

The people were finally at the border. Moses knew he wouldn't get to enter the land with them and so he shared his heart before he said good-bye. It was his last chance to remind his people of God's miraculous provision and of the journey on which He had led them. Moses' last words to his people make up the bulk of Deuteronomy.

Put Yourself in Their Sandals

Think about it! A whole generation passed while they were traveling in this gypsy-type of environment. Here's one way to look at it.

Let's say you were eight years old when the people left Egypt. You would have left Egypt with your parents and grandparents. By the time you were ten you would have traveled to the border of your destination. Then, when

PLAYING THE GAME OF REMEMBER WHEN. . .

You know how it is. You sit around with friends and tell stories you have all lived through, just for the fun of reliving them. Remember when we thought we were buying plaster to fix the wall and it was cement instead? Remember when Uncle Dan dressed up for a masquerade party as a go-go dancer and construction workers whistled at him? Remember when we got goofy at the wedding reception and laughed punch right out of our noses?

The remember whens for the Hebrews were on a little grander scale, but Moses was still creating the same effect. Remember when God did this for us?

- Remember when the angel of death swept through Egypt but our sons were saved because of the lamb's blood on the doorpost?

- Remember when God literally pulled back the waters so we could cross the Red Sea?

- Remember when we needed food and it appeared like dew on the ground every morning?

- Remember when we needed water and it gushed right out of a hard rock?

- Remember when Moses came down from the mountain and his face glowed from God's presence?

- Remember when we made that gold calf idol and Moses was so angry he threw down the Ten Commandments tablets and broke them?

- Remember when we whined and complained and began to die of poisonous snakebites?

- Remember when we heard the report of the spies and were too scared to enter the land?

everyone got scared to cross the border, you would have started traveling again, like gypsies in the desert. You would grow to be a teenager, into your twenties, possibly marry and have kids, then into your thirties, then into your forties, losing your grandparents and then your parents along the way.

Finally when you are getting close to fifty years old, you return again to the border of that land. You are an adult now and you're back at the same place you were when you were ten years old. And somehow you have got to keep from making the same mistakes your parents did.

It DOES sound like a good time for a book like Deuteronomy, a book that says, "Okay, this is where we've come from and what we are about and where we are going. We've spent forty years making mistakes. Let's regroup and move ahead."

The Problem with the Israelites

The Israelites had a once-in-a-lifetime experience. There is probably no other time when God's presence was more evident every day. There was a pillar of fire and a cloud that led the people. They saw miracle after miracle food on the ground every morning, quails out of thin air, water out of rocks divine plagues and punishments. God was obviously present and working.

Yet the Israelites continued to doubt.

It would be easy to judge these people, to say they had it easy. After all, they didn't have to have a lot of faith; they could see God's actions right before their eyes.

The Israelites show us what we all are capable of: not trusting God even after He's proven Himself, and asking Him to continually prove Himself over again.

IN CONTEXT

It might have been easier to see God work, but the Israelites only show us basic human nature. Most of us have experienced some kind of answered prayer, only to worry during the next time of trouble whether God will answer us. Most of us have seen God work in some way, whether we called it a miracle, guidance, or intuition. Yet, we didn't trust that we'd ever see Him work again.

Moses' Death

Moses led an amazing life. He was one of the few Hebrew males his age to survive a royally decreed slaughter. He was raised in a palace when he should have been a slave. He spent forty years living in the desert in preparation for this journey and more than forty years wandering the desert during the journey.

He spent his life following God's call and leading his people from slavery to freedom and a land promised to them. But at the end of it all, he never set foot in that land. He first knew this would happen when God gave him a simple set of instructions and, for once, Moses didn't obey them. The people needed water and God told Moses to speak to a rock and water would come. In frustration and anger, though, Moses didn't just speak to the rock, he violently and angrily struck the rock. He took on himself what was only God's to do. He lost perspective.

We don't know for now why a man who did so many good things still had this one thing held against him. It's one of the questions we won't have answered for us in this life. But Moses lived a good life and was an honorable man. The Bible calls Moses the most humble man on earth.

HISTORY BOOKS

If the history books of the Old Testament were a movie series, they would be rated at least PG. It was a rough time for humanity. War was the way to gain land and power meant right. But even in the midst of the rough-hewn society of that day, God was working and people turned their hearts to Him.

These books show you a slice of life that historians call the Bronze Age and the Iron Age. It was a time of great advances, but a time very different from our world of roadside trash pickup and orthodontia. It was a time before anesthesia was developed or doctors had figured out that they needed to wash their hands to keep down infection. In the midst of all these differences, it is amazing to note that people still dealt with the same issues: faithfulness in marriage, fear that they weren't hearing God right and asking Him for confirmation, civil unrest, and disobedience. What you find in these pages when you look past the technological and sociological differences is that we still have a lot in common with these people and can learn from what they faced.

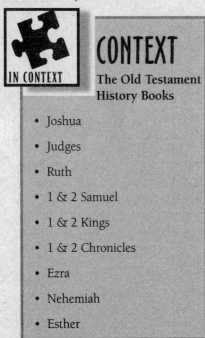

IN CONTEXT

CONTEXT

The Old Testament History Books

- Joshua

- Judges

- Ruth

- 1 & 2 Samuel

- 1 & 2 Kings

- 1 & 2 Chronicles

- Ezra

- Nehemiah

- Esther

JOSHUA

IN CONTEXT

Here's the scoop. . .

Written: *around 1370 B.C.*

Written by: *Joshua with the help of someone else.*

Writing style: *a chronological collection of true stories (war stories, mostly)*

One-liner: *The Hebrews resettled their land after over four hundred years away by facing down the squatters in every city.*

Joshua, the Soldier

After nearly forty more years of wandering, the Hebrews faced the border of their homeland for the second time. This time, though, they had a different kind of leader. God had given them Joshua, a soldier and a strategist.

The Book of Joshua is about the battles the Israelites waged to recapture and resettle their land. It involves a lot of force and a lot of blood. It involves a lot of actions that our present culture considers barbaric and violent. It was a barbaric and violent time. Basically, it's not a G-rated book. It's pretty violent.

Looking beyond the violence, though, it is a story of faith. When the people trusted in God's strength and obeyed His commands, they won their battles. When they didn't, they lost (and lost miserably). In this way, the Book of Joshua is relevant to the battles we face today in our lives, even though our weapons and our enemies look a lot different.

Truth Is Stranger Than Fiction

The Israelites won their battles as much by miracle as by strategy. Here are a few miraculous strategies God performed:

- They crossed a river—on dry ground. (Joshua 3:9–17)

- The people shouted, and the walls around a city fell down.
  (Joshua 6:1–27)

- God instructed Joshua to fake a retreat and stage an ambush! (Joshua 8:15–29)

- God won a battle using a hailstorm. (Joshua 10:6–11)

- The sun literally stood still so Joshua's army had more time to fight. (Joshua 10:13–14)

JUDGES

IN CONTEXT

Here's the scoop. . .

Written: *We don't know.*

Written by: *Maybe Samuel, but we're not sure.*

Writing style: *a collection of true stories*

One-liner: *The Hebrews organize into a nation back in their homeland and are led by wise judges.*

The Book of Judges

Before the Hebrews were slaves in Egypt, they were just a large family with twelve sons led by their father, Israel. When they left Egypt after generations of slavery, they were a people of 600,000+ adults led by a countryman, Moses. As they were settling into their homeland, they were led by a soldier, Joshua. Once they settled, they spent some time without any leadership at all. It was this period of time that the Book of Judges describes.

The era of the judges was an era of repeated cycles in the lives of the Israelites. They would fall away from God and fall prey to their enemies. When things got bad enough, they would turn back to God and He would raise up a leader, called a judge (often a military leader), who would rescue them from their current dilemma. But, as the cycle continued, the people would fall away again as soon as that judge had died or lost his influence. This cycle repeated itself through at least twelve different judges.

Deborah

Deborah is one of the most famous judges and the only one we know of that was a woman. She was wise and discerning and a prophet of God. She was known for holding court and settling disputes under a palm tree.

One day she informed Barak, a military leader, that he was to organize ten thousand men to wage a war. Barak refused to go to war unless Deborah accompanied him. Deborah's response was very interesting. She reminded Barak that if she went with him to war, the word would be spread that a woman won the battle. (Remember, this was a VERY sexist era. This interchange alone required Deborah and Barak to live above the culture of their day.)

Deborah did go to battle with Barak and they were victorious. Their song of victory is recorded in Judges 5.

Gideon

Gideon was an unlikely leader. He wasn't a member of an important family and he wasn't even an important member of his own family. But, God called him to lead and he obeyed.

Gideon started with thirty-two thousand men. Through God's leadership, he pared them down to just ten thousand. Through testing that ten thousand, he pared them down to just three hundred men. With just three hundred men, Gideon accomplished God's purposes.

At one point in Gideon's life, he needed to know God's direction, so he created a little test. He put a fleece of wool out on the ground overnight and asked God to let dew fall on the fleece but not on the ground. God did it. The next night Gideon asked God to let dew fall on the ground, but not on the fleece. God did it. Today people still talk about putting a fleece out before God to determine a specific answer or to "find His will" about something. When they do, they are referring to Gideon.

Samson

Samson was, perhaps, the most famous judge. He grew to be the strongest man in the country. His strength was founded on a special commitment he had made to God, called a Nazirite commitment. Part of this promise required that the Nazirite never cut his hair. As long as Samson kept this commitment, his strength stayed with him.

He got involved with a woman named Delilah, though, who tricked him into cutting his hair. Samson's life went from bad to worse from then on. He was blinded and kept as a slave. He eventually killed his captors, but he died along with them.

RUTH

IN CONTEXT

Here's the scoop. . .

Written: *around 1350 B.C.*

Written by: *Some people think Samuel wrote part of it, but we don't know for sure.*

Writing style: *a true story about a Jewish family*

One-liner: *one family's story about God's provision*

A Love Story

The Book of Ruth is about love on a lot of different levels. The story opens with a woman, Naomi, her husband, and her two sons leaving their home because of famine. They settled in a land called Moab. There the two boys married. (Their wives were named Orpah and Ruth.) Naomi, Orpah, and Ruth all became widows. After the deaths of her husband and her sons, Naomi decided to go back to her hometown and freed her daughters-in-law to go and make their own lives in their own land.

After much protesting, Naomi finally convinced Orpah to leave, but Ruth would not budge from Naomi's side. She committed to building her life with Naomi. Together they traveled back to Bethlehem. Their experiences there are told in the Book of Ruth.

The Rest of the Story

After settling in Bethlehem, Ruth went out to gather leftover wheat from the fields surrounding Bethlehem. She was noticed by a distant relative of Naomi named Boaz. According to Jewish laws, he could marry Ruth and at the same time actually be honoring a family obligation.

That's exactly what happened. Ruth and Boaz married and gave Naomi a grandchild. And (get a load of this), it was through their family line that the famous King David as well as Jesus Christ was born.

1 SAMUEL

Here's the scoop...

Written: *during King David's reign*

Written by: *Samuel, Nathan, and Gad*

Writing style: *a historical account*

One-liner: *Samuel leads Israel, then he anoints King Saul, then he anoints King David.*

First, the Story of a Priest

Samuel was a miracle baby. His mother had been infertile and prayed long and hard for a child. Because she was so aware that her child was a gift from God, when he was old enough, she sent him to live at the temple to be raised and apprenticed by Eli, the priest.

When Samuel grew up, he was the leader of Israel. But, what Israel wanted was a king. A king?!? This would change everything about Israel's government. They had only been ruled by God and then a few judges (see the Book of Judges). Samuel tried to dissuade them, but Israel demanded. They wanted to be like all the other countries around them (a logic you might recognize from an argument with a middle-schooler). So it was Samuel who anointed their first and second kings.

Then, the Story of a King

The first king of Israel was a young man named Saul. He had a lot going for him and did many great things for Israel. He was committed to God...at first. Then he wavered, then he fell, then he literally went insane.

During King Saul's most troubled moments, he was calmed by a young musician named David. (Do you remember that old spiritual "Play on Your Harp, Little David"?) David became best friends with Jonathan, Saul's son. Little did Saul know that because he had stopped obeying God, he would one day be replaced by David.

As Saul began to realize David's growing popularity, he became jealous and angry and increasingly distressed. He treated David like an outlaw. King Saul finally died in a battle along with his son Jonathan (David's best friend).

Then, the Story of Another King

David was anointed future king while he was still a young and very unlikely candidate. He was anointed by Samuel after God rejected Saul as the rightful king.

Soon after, David was honored with the opportunity to play music before King Saul. The king was so impressed with him that he made David an armor-bearer. This is how it came to be that David was at the camp when Goliath made his challenge. You probably remember the story about little David taking his slingshot out to meet the giant, Goliath, and killing him with one stone.

This was the beginning of David's leadership, but it was the beginning of the end for Saul's. As the story of David and Goliath grew, the people of Israel started comparing David and Saul. Eventually Saul resented it so much that David was left a refugee, an outlaw, wandering from cave to cave trying to survive against Saul's anger and his armies.

When Saul was killed in battle, David sincerely grieved for him. Then David took over the throne.

2 SAMUEL

IN CONTEXT

Here's the scoop. . .

Written: *just after King David's reign*

Written by: *Probably by Nathan and Gad. Possibly other writers contributed.*

Writing style: *a historical account*

One-liner: *King David reigns and his family suffers.*

Story of a Monarchy

The Book of 2 Samuel is a continuation of the story begun in the Book of 1 Samuel. At the end of 1 Samuel, King Saul had been killed in battle and King David had taken the throne. Second Samuel is all about King David's monarchy.

The Rise of David

David was an interesting character. The only other person the Bible has more stories about is Jesus Christ. David was a great man, but not always a good one. He often stood for right, but he often failed as a husband and father.

The first ten chapters of 2 Samuel are about the great things that King David did. He built a strong and prosperous kingdom. He returned the ark of the covenant to the tabernacle. He made plans to build a temple. He kept a lifelong promise to his best friend Jonathan (who died in battle with King Saul) and took care of Jonathan's physically challenged son.

The Fall of David

David's most famous mistake (and the beginning of his fall from power) was an affair he had with a married woman named Bathsheba. First, David pursued her, slept with her, and then found out she had become pregnant. Next he tried to get her husband, Uriah, home from war so it would look like the baby was his. Poor Uriah (besides having an awful name by today's standards) so revered the king that he wouldn't even go home and enjoy being with his wife while he was on leave.

Next, David set Uriah up to be killed in battle. So David was guilty of adultery, attempted paternity fraud, and murder—all from seeing someone bathing and giving in to temptation. This is a king?

David ended up making Bathsheba his wife, but the baby died. They later had more children—including the future king, Solomon.

David's Dysfunctional Family

After David's affair with Bathsheba, his life only went from bad to worse. His children by his first wives were out of control. One son, Amnon, raped his half-sister, Tamar. Another son, Absalom (who had supermodel good looks and long hair), killed Amnon because of the rape. Eventually Absalom rebelled against his father. He was killed by King David's men when they found him hanging from a tree limb by his hair. His mule had ridden under the tree and when Absalom's hair caught in the limbs, the mule just kept on going (yes, it really happened). It almost sounds like an R-rated black comedy, doesn't it?

David's throne was succeeded by his son Solomon. Solomon was the second-born son of Bathsheba and grew to be a wise and wealthy king.

THINK ABOUT IT THIS WAY

One of the most important things to know about David is that God called him "a man after his own heart" (1 Samuel 13:14). As you have read, David's life was far from perfect. Because of that he is a great example to us that God desires our faith and it is on the basis of that faith that He approves of us. Then He walks with us through our mistakes and failures, redeeming us on the basis of that faith.

1 KINGS

IN CONTEXT

Here's the scoop. . .

Written: *We don't know.*

Written by: *Perhaps a group of people, but we don't know for sure.*

Writing style: *a historical account*

One-liner: *King Solomon reigns, and then the kingdom divides into the northern and southern kingdoms.*

The Story Line

The Book of 1 Kings opens with the death of the great King David. Before he died, David named one of his sons, Solomon, as his successor. The first half of 1 Kings is about Solomon's establishing his kingdom, building the temple, and amassing his un-i-MAG-in-able wealth.

The second half of 1 Kings is about the kingdom after Solomon. Things get a little complicated here, so hang on tight. The one kingdom of Israel divides into two kingdoms—Israel (the northern kingdom, later called Samaria) and Judah (the southern kingdom). It was an ongoing civil war.

King Solomon

Solomon was known for his wisdom. In fact, God appeared to Solomon in a dream and told him to ask for anything he wanted. (Who wouldn't love to be in that dream? The God of all creation offering you anything. . . .) Solomon's request was a surprising one. He asked for wisdom to rule well and to know right from wrong. God rewarded such a request by giving Solomon not only wisdom and understanding, but also the wealth and honor that he could have asked for but didn't.

One of the first things Solomon did as king was build a beautiful temple. Solomon then built his own palace (took thirteen years) and continued to amass amazing wealth. Sounds great, right? Well, there was one little problem.

One Little Problem

Way back when, Solomon had married a foreigner, a girl from Egypt (where his forefathers had been slaves, you might note). Along with this wife came her religious practices of worshiping idols. He also married many other women who worshiped other gods. Wouldn't you know it, while things were going great for Solomon, he got more and more tolerant of these idol-worship practices until he was worshiping false gods! It was like spitting in the face of God Almighty.

By the end of Solomon's life, he was a disillusioned old man. He had let go of his foundation and his kingdom went downhill after him.

The Divided Kingdom

You might remember that the origin of the twelve tribes of Israel was the twelve sons of Jacob, whom God renamed Israel. They all traveled to Egypt and then traveled back to the land of, you got it, Israel. One tribe, the descendants of Levi, were given no land because they were the priests and would work in the temple rather than work the land. The land was divided among the other tribes.

After Solomon's death, a civil conflict broke out. The northern tribes followed a man named Jeroboam. The southern tribes, Benjamin and Judah, continued to follow Solomon's son Rehoboam. They never reunited.

Ahab and Jezebel

One of the most famous kings of the northern kingdom of Israel was Ahab. You've probably heard of King Ahab and his wife, Queen Jezebel. You may have even heard of someone referred to as a jezebel. If so, you probably steered clear of her. Jezebel was a mess. She was the Cruella DeVille of her day. If she had lived in the southern kingdom, she'd have probably been called a "floozy." Ahab wasn't a lot better, but he didn't come across as quite so conniving. You know…behind every bad man, there is usually a worse woman.

Ahab reigned for twenty-two years. The Bible says he made the sins of the former kings look trivial. In fact, the Bible says that Ahab did more to provoke God's anger than all the kings before him. He and his wife reveled

IN CONTEXT

It might sound like things had really changed for the people of Israel (who are now known as the people of Israel and the people of Judah), but in reality it was the same song, second verse. They still fell away from God until they got into trouble and then ran back to Him for help. God forgave and helped them, but He didn't protect them from consequences, and by the end of the story, those consequences were pretty grim.

in the worship of Baal. They were downright zealous about it. Basically they encouraged evil as much as they could.

There was one man who stood in their way. An important player in the story of 1 Kings is the prophet Elijah, a beacon in that dark day and an aggravating flea in Jezebel's proverbial mane.

Elijah

Elijah was a Tishbite (funny word, say it out loud). He was from a place called Tishbe. He first appeared when he announced to King Ahab that God was about to declare a drought.

Elijah didn't always come out on top. Once, in particular, he got the "poor-me-willies" when he had worked really hard to confront evil and all he got for it was run out of town. But, most often, Elijah had great faith and God used him and provided for him in miraculous ways. He was fed by ravens once. Another time, a widow's flour and oil were miraculously replenished because she fed him. It was even through Elijah that a woman's son was brought back to life. But there is definitely one miracle that is Elijah's all-time claim to fame.

The Big Showdown

Elijah invited Ahab and Jezebel's false religion to a showdown once. It was on top of Mt. Carmel. He instructed the prophets of Baal (an idol) to build an altar, place a sacrifice there, and to pray to their god to send down fire to light the altar. Elijah built an altar as well and soaked it in barrels and barrels of water.

As you can imagine, the Baal prophets prayed and danced and shouted and even (yes, really) cut themselves to show their fervor and sincerity. But when you are praying to nothing, nothing happens. No fire from heaven. Only a lot of bleeding prophets and some very raw meat.

Then Elijah prayed over his wet, soggy sacrifice of an altar. God responded. Fire came down from heaven and consumed that altar, the sacrifice, and the water.

It was a good day for God's people. It was a bad day for Baal's prophets (who were chased down and killed). And, boy, was Jezebel mad.

2 KINGS

Here's the scoop. . .

Written: *No one knows.*

Written by: *We don't know for sure. It may have been a group of writers.*

Writing style: *a historical account*

One-liner: *the story of the divided kingdoms of Israel and Judah during the time of Elijah and Elisha*

A Nation Divided

The Book of 2 Kings is a sequel to 1 Kings. Israel had divided into two kingdoms (northern: Israel; southern: Judah) with their own separate kings, separate economies, separate worships, and separate problems.

Throughout the different governments, God sent prophets to call the people back to obedience. Unfortunately, they continued to return to idolatry. In the end, each kingdom fell. The northern kingdom fell to the Assyrians and the southern kingdom fell to the Babylonians.

Two Good Kings

There were two kings in the southern kingdom that tried to get their country back in line. The first was Hezekiah. One of his first official acts was to restore and open the temple and to destroy the idol altars and worship center. One of his biggest contributions was to create an aqueduct system so that water came within Jerusalem's city walls (so that during battle they could survive without having to leave the city).

The second righteous king was Josiah. Josiah was crowned king at the age of eight. He also restored the temple and, in doing so, found an old copy of the Book of the Law (probably Deuteronomy). Because of this book, Josiah called himself and his people to a new level of understanding and obedience. Josiah was killed in battle at only thirty-nine years of age.

Prophets

During Israel and Judah's time of falling away from God, they were consistently reminded of their mistakes by prophets. These men sometimes foretold the future, but also just told the truth. They spoke with the kings. They were known throughout the land. Often they were respected as well as abused.

One of the most famous prophets was Elijah. Elijah left the earth not through death but through a chariot of fire (a story you allude to every time you sing "Swing low, sweet chariot, comin' for to carry me home").

Elijah's apprentice prophet was Elisha. Elisha lived an honorable life and even established a school for prophets.

IN CONTEXT

The work of some of the other prophets of that era is recorded in actual books of the Bible such as Isaiah, Micah, Hosea, and Jeremiah. God showed His love by never giving up on His people. He kept calling them back through the message of the prophets, but they never got it together enough to follow Him consistently.

1 CHRONICLES

IN CONTEXT

Here's the scoop. . .

Written: *around 400 B.C.*

Written by: *Ezra, according to Jewish tradition*

Writing style: *some historical accounts and some lists of genealogies*

One-liner: *Israel's story from David's reign but from a spiritual, rather than political view*

A Sense of Roots in a Dark Time

The Book of 1 Chronicles was written at a time in Israel's history when the people had been physically displaced from their homes. After their exile, they came back home to find that their land had been settled by foreigners. They needed to reunite as a people and reconnect with God. First Chronicles was written to help them do that.

Genealogies

The Book of 1 Chronicles opens with lists upon lists of genealogies. In fact, there are eight chapters of these lists. True, they are not enthralling bedtime reading fare, but look at them through the eyes of the original readers. This was a culture in which individuals defined themselves by their family history. Their land was even parceled out according to which of the twelve sons of Israel their family descended from. Their whole identity was in genealogies. Their way of life, for the most part, was passed on through stories, oral traditions, feasts, and holidays that found their origin in the great deliverance from Egypt (see Exodus for clarification on that one).

IN CONTEXT

While you may not read all of the genealogies in 1 Chronicles word for word, understand that to these people these lists were the only roots they had. Their homes were reinhabited; their land was full of squatters. All that defined them as a nation were the names you see in 1 Chronicles and the lives those names represented. First Chronicles gets a bad rap for having some yawn material, but when you understand where these people were as a nation, you understand that they weren't yawning when they wrote it.

Israel's Family History

The largest part of 1 Chronicles is a different kind of history. It describes many of the same events you find in 2 Samuel and in 1 and 2 Kings. There is a much different perspective on those events, though. First Chronicles was written many years after these events. Whenever you look at a period of time from the vantage point of "many years later," you see things differently. You see more of the highlights than the details. You see the significance rather than just the events themselves. First Chronicles really describes the history of worship in Israel, the history of their relationship with God, rather than just who ruled when and for how long.

King David

David is the central character in 1 Chronicles. As a king, David did many things, but this book describes in detail his temple preparations.

David focused the pre-exile Israelites on worship. Because of this, it was a good thing for the post-exile Israelites to look back again on David's role in history so that they could, once again, make worship a priority. Their temple lay in ruins. Their homes weren't much better. In 1 Chronicles they could find a pattern to follow to find their roots in their family and in their religious commitment.

Accomplishments

When we look back on our lives, or anybody's life, we can see a clear path of what they accomplished. But when we are in the middle of living our lives, sometimes the path is not so clear. We can't know what King David was thinking about worship in his day, but looking back, it's as if he had this plan in mind:

- Recapture Jerusalem so I can put the temple there.
- Return the ark of the covenant (the most holy thing in Jewish history, sort of like a holy time capsule) to the tabernacle. (The tabernacle was the portable precursor to the temple.)
- Write songs for the tabernacle choir to sing and work with the choir director, Asaph.
- Organize the priests, the worship musicians, and the guards.
- Gather together building supplies and equipment so that when the time is right, Solomon, my son, can build the temple.

If David had a to-do list, it must have looked something like this because this is exactly what he did.

2 CHRONICLES

Here's the scoop. . .

Written: *around 400 B.C.*

Written by: *Ezra, according to Jewish tradition*

Writing style: *a historical account*

One-liner: *Israel's story from Solomon's reign into the divided kingdom from a spiritual perspective*

A Nation in Review

The Book of 2 Chronicles is a continuation of 1 Chronicles. So, like 1 Chronicles, it is a recounting of the historical events listed in 1 and 2 Kings, but from a very different perspective. Second Chronicles is written many years later (than Kings) and in the rearview. The Jewish people have been away from their land in exile and are just returning. They have been lost and wandering with no roots and no familiarity.

The writer of the Chronicles (probably Ezra, according to tradition) set about to give the people a sense of history and identity. In light of this, the Chronicles place more emphasis on the positive aspects of the historical characters. There were many wicked and idolatrous kings in the history of Judah, but the Chronicles bring out the best in the reign of these men. It is a deliberate attempt to remind Israel of what they can be proud of and hold on to about their history. It is also a reminder of how their forefathers served and worshiped God, so that they can start their new life at home on the right foot.

TABLOIDS

Here are some of the headlines you would read if
2 Chronicles had a tabloid following:

- Great King Solomon reduces silver to the worth of a
  stone (2 Chronicles 1)

- Royal grandmother kills all her descendants so she
  can become queen (2 Chronicles 22)

- Child-king crowned at the age of seven
  (2 Chronicles 24)

- Ahaz, national leader, involved in child sacrifice
  (2 Chronicles 28)

- King Jehoahaz sets record for shortest reign
  (2 Chronicles 36)

Solomon

The reign of Solomon takes up the first portion of 2 Chronicles. Solomon
was wise. He was wealthy. He was influential. He had many wives. He had it
all. In his younger years, it served him well. In his older years, it disillusioned him. In fact he wrote a book of the Bible named Ecclesiastes in
which he says he'd had it all and without God "all" means nothing.

The Kings of Judah

After Solomon's reign, the kingdom was divided into the southern kingdom,
Judah, and the northern kingdom, Israel. Second Chronicles concentrates
on the rulers of Judah. Of those rulers, 2 Chronicles draws a direct correla-
tion between their commitment to God and the success of their kingdom.
Throughout their history God told them, "Obey me and I will bless you,
disobey me and you will not succeed." Second Chronicles reveals in hindsight that what God said was true.

EZRA

IN CONTEXT

Here's the scoop. . .

Written: *around 400 B.C.*

Written by: *probably Ezra*

Writing style: *a historical account*

One-liner: *The Hebrews returned from Babylonian exile and rebuilt the temple.*

The Main Gist

You may or may not remember that at the end of 2 Chronicles the Hebrews had been exiled to Babylon. When the Persians then invaded Babylon, the Persian leader, Cyrus, let the Jewish people return home. This was a good and a bad thing. They had been in Babylon SEVENTY YEARS! Many of the people who first came had died. More than a whole generation had made their home in Persia. Jerusalem, their hometown, was nine hundred miles away and this was before automobiles. (Even in a car on a highway, nine hundred miles takes around fifteen hours. Can you imagine on foot?) There was a reluctance among many Hebrews to take Cyrus up on his offer.

Exiles Return with Zerubbabel

Out of two million, about fifty thousand did choose to travel back to their homeland with a man named Zerubbabel (zuh-RU-buh-bul). Their priority when they got there was to rebuild the temple. The significance of this act was more than just having a place to worship. It was an act of restructuring their relationship with God.

There was a great celebration when the builders completed the foundation. There was music and cheering and worship. And there was sadness, too. The senior citizens who had returned with Zerubbabel could remember the grand and glorious temple that Solomon built. They wept at how far they had fallen away from those days.

IN CONTEXT

The history of these people had been a very on-again, off-again style of worship. The fact that they traveled home and rebuilt the temple was a sign that they acknowledged God's leadership in the life of their nation. This was a big step.

Exiles Return with Ezra

After the temple had been rebuilt, Ezra returned to Jerusalem with about two thousand more people (many of them priests). What he found disappointed him. The temple was together, but was so much less grand than before.

Ezra's main concern wasn't the building, though. The temple's poor condition was just a reflection of the poor condition of the people's hearts. This really grieved Ezra. He had a vision for restoring his people. He tore his clothes (which was a sign of grief and despair in those days). He preached his heart out. And it worked! The people renewed their relationship with God.

There's Always a Snag in Construction

Even as long ago as this book records, people used paperwork to delay construction. Observe this scenario from Ezra 4.

- Now, remember, there was no e-mail, no fax, no phone, no carbons, no copiers, not even any postal service. There were only camels, chariots, and messengers. And there were nine hundred miles between the building site and the capital city of the government. (You think YOU had delays!)

- Hostile neighbors offered to "help" with construction of the temple. The Israelites refused their help. The neighbors took the attitude of "We'll show them. . . ."

- The neighbors sent messengers or agents with lies about the Israelites. They sent these stories back to King Cyrus as long as he reigned, then King Darius after him. After Darius, they wrote to Ahasuerus and then

King Artaxerxes. They warned the kings that the Hebrews were trouble and if the construction continued, they'd probably stop paying taxes. (Ouch. That must have hurt! Hit 'em right in the tax treasury.)

- King Artaxerxes looked up in his files the history of Judah and Israel and saw their history of rebellion. That wasn't reassuring, so he sent back a demand (nine hundred miles again) for the reconstruction to stop.

- In the midst of this, the Israelites began to fight fire with fire. They began construction again and wrote to the king asking him to look back in his files one more time and find the ORIGINAL decree from King Cyrus authorizing the construction. Off went the secretaries to search through the parchment and stone tablets and there it was, dust and all. (No building permit EVER took this much work.)

- Construction resumed and the file clerk took a break.

Now THAT, my friends, is bureaucracy—multigenerational bureaucracy.

NEHEMIAH

IN CONTEXT

Here's the scoop. . .

Written: *around 400 B.C.*

Written by: *Ezra and Nehemiah may have written this together.*

Writing style: *a historical account*

One-liner: *More Hebrews returned from Babylon and rebuilt Jerusalem's wall.*

Nehemiah Takes a Risk

Talk about a career strategy. Nehemiah was a man who believed in a creative job market. As the story opens, Nehemiah is a cupbearer to the king. Part of his job was typical administrative assistant kind of stuff and part was butlering. But part of his job was, literally, to taste the king's wine. One reason was quality control. The other was poison control. Talk about living on the edge!

The good thing about Nehemiah's job was that it gave him opportunities to talk directly with the king about his concerns. Nehemiah had heard from a friend that the Jewish people who had left Babylon to rebuild Jerusalem were having a bad time. The city walls were destroyed and this left the city open to attack. This news broke Nehemiah's heart.

When the king asked why Nehemiah seemed so sad (a sensitive boss!), there was a ready response. Nehemiah asked for a leave of absence to help build the wall. He got the time off from work and headed to Jerusalem.

Nehemiah Builds a Wall

A couple of days after his arrival, Nehemiah snuck out at night and surveyed the wall. It was a mess.

To understand why he had to sneak around, you have to understand that this land had been inhabited by so many people that there were mixed feelings in regard to the Hebrews' reinhabiting the land. There were also government officials who were very sensitive to any independence the Hebrews might regain that would cause them to rebel or (tell me no!) stop paying taxes.

Once Nehemiah had seen the wall, he announced his plan. He divided the gates and sections of the wall among different people and set them to work. Most of the people were glad to be working. Then again, there were two characters named Sanballat and Tobiah.

Sanballat and Tobiah were threatened by the whole resettlement thing. They feared they would lose their own power over the people. So, their first strategy was intimidation and verbal abuse.

Nehemiah prayed.

Then they tried to discourage the workers.

Nehemiah reminded them of God's help.

Then they sank to a new level of threats of physical abuse.

Nehemiah armed the workers and set up battle strategies with them. Basically the builders had a tool in one hand and weapon in the other. What a way to build a wall!

Finally, Sanballat and Tobiah threatened to assassinate Nehemiah.

Nehemiah prayed again, but he didn't back down.

Believe it or not, those builders finished that wall in less than two months (actually fifty-two days, about seven weeks). This was no small feat considering that it was such a sturdy, wide wall that when they finished, they marched on top of it around the city to celebrate. (Can you imagine that party scene?)

Revival Meeting

After the completion of the wall, Ezra (same guy from the Book of Ezra) read the Law of God to the people. Together they confessed their sin and recommitted themselves to follow God and to worship Him, to take care of the temple, and to, basically, clean up their act.

Nehemiah worked for a long time to help the Hebrews renew and maintain their commitment to God's way of doing things.

THINK ABOUT IT THIS WAY

SPEAKER FOR HIRE

If Nehemiah were living today, he would be a prime candidate to speak at leadership conferences. He was an excellent leader and administrator. If he gave you a handout, his main points would look something like this:

- Pray for wisdom about decisions and opportunities.
- If at all possible, work through the powers that be, the chain of command.
- Survey your task well before beginning work.
- Divide your task into manageable segments and then assign it to someone who has an interest in its completion.
- Don't give in to bullies.
- Don't let someone threaten your reputation. Stand on your own integrity.
- Confront problems and people head-on.
- Know what the Bible says and follow its advice.

ESTHER

Here's the scoop. . .

Written: *around 500 B.C.*

Written by: *We're not sure.*

Writing style: *a story of a queen*

One-liner: *The Hebrews survived exile in Persia because of a Jewish "royal beauty contest" winner.*

Generally Speaking

Esther is a story that shows God at work in everyday circumstances. It's a story that affirms for us that coincidences, most often, are not a matter of chance at all.

The events of Esther happened in Babylon while the Hebrews were in captivity there. They weren't slaves; they were forced immigrants. They could do business and live their lives, but they weren't citizens of Babylon. They were waiting to go home someday.

Queen Vashti

The story opens with a conflict between King Ahasuerus (also called Xerxes) and Queen Vashti. The king was having a wild and raucous party with his friends and called for his wife so he could show off her beauty. The queen refused to come. REFUSED TO COME!?! That might not seem like a big deal today, but in that day, it was a very big deal. In fact, such a big deal that the king divorced her and opened up a search, a beauty contest of sorts, for a new queen.

That event set the stage for Esther's story.

Enter: Esther

Esther was a beautiful girl. She was a Jewish girl (her Jewish name was
Hadassah). She was also an orphan, so her older cousin, Mordecai, was like
a father to her. Mordecai entered Esther in the contest. She won and sure
enough rose above the ranks and married the king. Somehow this all happened without the king's knowing she was Jewish.

Everything went along fine until…Haman.

Haman's Plan

Haman was a Hitler wanna-be. He was a power-hungry fellow who would
be happy to exterminate the Hebrews from his country. He was a bigot, a
racist, a bully. He particularly disliked Esther's cousin, Mordecai. Mordecai
had won the king's favor by uncovering an assassination plot, thus saving
the king. Haman didn't like Mordecai's good name one little bit, and it
didn't help matters that Mordecai was not a man who bowed down before
Haman. Haman made a plan to be rid of the Jewish people with Mordecai at
the top of the hit list.

But, what Haman didn't realize was that the queen was not only Hebrew,
but was related to the man he was preparing to assassinate. Mordecai went
to Esther so that she could talk to the king on his behalf and save her people. This was a scary thing for Esther (it was against the law to approach the
king uninvited), but she did it. In fact, she revealed Haman's plot to the
king with Haman right there in the room.

The End

By the end, justice was done. Haman was hanged on his own gallows. His
plan was nixed. Mordecai was honored by the king. Esther remained queen
but no longer had to keep her nationality a secret. The Jewish people established a new feast, Purim. Even today when a Hebrew family celebrates
Purim, they read together the story of Esther and celebrate God's salvation
through their very own Queen of Persia.

WISDOM BOOKS

These books are like poetry. They are writings more than they are books. They are collections of thoughts. They are lyrics. They are creativity from an ancient world. They are right-brainers relating to God and all of us getting to listen in.

IN CONTEXT

Wisdom Books

- Job

- Psalms

- Proverbs

- Ecclesiastes

- Song of Solomon

JOB

IN CONTEXT

Here's the scoop. . .

Written: *No one is sure, but the story probably happened around 2000 B.C.*

Written by: *Job might have written, but we don't know.*

Writing style: *an ancient Hebrew poem (It didn't rhyme, though.)*

One-liner: *Bad times don't mean that God isn't good; they just mean that some times are bad.*

A Peek Behind Eternity's Curtain

We don't often think of God and Satan sitting down for a chat. We know they were once companions. Satan was an angel, for goodness' sake, but then things changed, not for goodness' sake.

We may not think about God and Satan communicating, but that was exactly the way the Book of Job began. Satan was talking to God about Job. He made the accusation that Job was only faithful to God because Job had a good life. God denied that was true and, in so many words, told Satan to go ahead and give it his best shot.

Then Job began to suffer. He suffered loss and illness and poverty and, worst of all, three well-meaning friends.

Job's "Friends"

At first Job's friends sat with him, offering comfort with their presence. But eventually they did what so many well-meaning people do when they are around suffering. They tried to figure out why it was happening. And ultimately they came to the question we all come to, "What did Job do to deserve this?"

Even sick, having lost his children and his wealth, everything except his despairing wife, Job stood firm. He had done nothing to deserve all this. That left them with the only other question they could ask, "If he doesn't deserve it, then why is it happening?" Since there was no answer to that question, they just kept badgering Job to 'fess up. Then finally God spoke.

God's Reasoning

The bottom line of God's response was, "Who do you think you are?" (a question that we can never answer without first visiting, "Who do we think God is?"). God reestablished His place in the world, His creation, His sovereignty, His power, His desire for righteousness from people.

God doesn't answer the question of why there is evil and suffering in the world. Probably because it was answered in the first three chapters of Genesis (humanity brought it on by bad choices). But God does say that He is the same when we are suffering or when we aren't. He is loving when we are blessed and He is loving when we are cursed. Our suffering is not a product of His punishment or a way in which His feelings have changed about us. Life is simply a suffering place sometimes.

This is still difficult for us to understand mainly because sometimes God intervenes and keeps our suffering from us—but sometimes He doesn't. And in the end, whether we understand or not, His being able to make that choice is why we call Him God.

PSALMS

IN CONTEXT

Here's the scoop. . .

Written: *over a span of time, anywhere from 1400–500 B.C.*

Written by: *a variety of authors including David, Asaph, Solomon, and Moses*

Writing style: *poetry and song lyrics*

One-liner: *lyric sheets from Old Testament temple handbook*

In General

The Book of Psalms is a collection of poems. Most of these poems are also lyrics to a song. Some historians call this book the "Book of Praises." Others call it the Greek name, "Psalmoi," which means "twangings" (like on a harp). Still others call it the Psaltery, which comes from "Psalterion" (songs to be played with a harp). Some just call it "the hymnbook of Solomon's temple."

In Specific

The topics of Psalms include:

- God's goodness
- God's protection
- God's love
- Anger
- Jealousy
- Joy
- Regret
- Enemies
- The wonder of life
- Fear
- Praises
- Funeral dirges

But They Don't Rhyme

What's that you say? If they are songs, if they are lyrics, if they are poems, why don't they rhyme? Well, since they were written in another language, one might assume that they rhymed in the other language, just not in English. No. The style of poetry at that time in the Hebrew culture and language was a whole different way of thinking. Their music was not based on three chords and a chorus the way Western music is today.

THINK ABOUT IT THIS WAY

There are 150 songs in Psalms. Some are about God and some are addressed to God. Some are gloriously happy and worshipful, and some are filled with dejection and rage. The psalms were what any songbook should be, a collection of the innermost feelings of people. They are honest. They are full of real life-prayers. They are rubber-meets-the-road, real-life thoughts of people who struggled and celebrated the same things that every person does, but in the end remained in God's presence.

Their poetry forms were based on the thoughts in the poems. The first line usually expressed the central thought. Then the second line repeated or built on that thought. Often each line then continued to build, but on that same central thought. For instance Psalm 27 builds this way:

The LORD is my light and my salvation;
Whom shall I fear?
   The LORD is the strength of my life;
   Of whom shall I be afraid?
When the wicked came against me
To eat up my flesh,
My enemies and foes,
They stumbled and fell.
   Though an army may encamp against me,
   My heart shall not fear; though war may rise against me,
   In this I will be confident.

                          (Psalm 27:1–3 NKJV)

Does Anyone Here Play an Instrument?

Today an orchestra is made up of strings, woodwinds, percussions, some brass, etc. A band is made up of drums, guitars, sometimes keyboards. Musical instruments were used with the Jewish "church services," as well.

Cymbals—There were two types of cymbals: The clashing cymbals were large disks. The resounding cymbals were small disks attached to the thumb and the middle finger.

Flute—Also called a shepherd's pipe. Smaller than the oboe and without a reed.

Harp—This was a twelve-stringed instrument, held vertically and played with the fingers.

Horns—Also called trumpets, these instruments were made of rams' horns or of hammered metal. They called the people to worship. (They also were the instruments used when the people shouted and the walls of Jericho fell down.)

Lyre—Smaller than the harp, with only ten strings and plucked with a pick. Our modern hammered dulcimer is a distant cousin of the lyre.

Oboe—Often translated as flute or pipe, the word *chalil* means an instrument with double reeds, like an oboe.

Rattle—Also called a sistrum. Often these were made of clay with stones inside to make the rattling rhythm sound. Today similar shakers used are made out of plastic or wood and shaped like eggs.

Tambourine—Round like our modern tambourines, but with no "jingles" on the side. This tambourine was used as a small drum.

Dancing Before There Were Discotheques

Not only were musical instruments used in the worship services of ancient Israel, but dance also was an integral part of worship and of ceremonies. David danced before the Lord. Miriam danced during a celebration.

The movements were certainly different and were not sexual in nature, but movement was an important part of celebrating the God who gives life. Go ahead and try it. Think about your blessings and do a little jig.

PROVERBS

IN CONTEXT

Here's the scoop. . .

Written: *around 950 B.C.*

Written by: *several writers including Solomon, Agur, and Lemuel*

Writing style: *a collection of wise sayings, some in the form of Hebrew poetry*

One-liner: *nuggets of wisdom for dealing with everyday life*

Solomon's Wisdom

The Book of Proverbs is a collection of wise sayings. It's almost like a bag of godly-wisdom-fortune-cookies, minus the cookies, plus the wisdom (minus the numbers on the back that nobody knows what they mean). These Proverbs are a good example of Hebrew poetry. Many are couplets (two lines) that express the same thought two different ways. Sometimes they restate and sometimes they give examples by stating the opposite.

Proverbial Examples

The fear of the LORD is the beginning of knowledge:
    but fools despise wisdom and instruction. (Proverbs 1:7 KJV)

(See, the second line is the opposite of the first line.)

My son, pay attention to what I say; listen closely to my words.
    Do not let them out of your sight, keep them within your heart.
    (Proverbs 4:20–21)

(The second line restates the first lines.)

Many are the plans in a man's heart,
    but it is the LORD's purpose that prevails. (Proverbs 19:21)

THINK ABOUT IT THIS WAY

USING THIS BOOK

Some people read a chapter of Proverbs every day month after month. Since it's broken into thirty-one chapters, there is a daily reading that correlates with every day of the month. Proverbs is a hodgepodge of truth, but it is a precious book, because you can always find something there that will affect your choices on that very day. It's a book about how you live your life in the details where things can get the most complicated.

Handouts

If you were teaching a seminar based on the Book of Proverbs, here are some of the sessions you might include:

- God's Perspective on Sex

- Having Friends

- Knowing God

- Leadership, God's Way

- Loving Things or Loving People?

- Making Sense of Marriage and Family Issues

- Money Management

- Morality and You

- Time Management

- Using Words Wisely

- Working for a Living

ECCLESIASTES

IN CONTEXT

Here's the scoop...

Written: *around 900 B.C.*

Written by: *probably Solomon*

Writing style: *wisdom literature, which means a profound kind of thought-provoking writing, sometimes called poetry*

One-liner: *I've had it all, and it didn't mean anything without God. Sincerely, King Solomon*

The Man Who Had It All

Remember Solomon? He was King David's son. When he was a young king, God asked him what he wanted, and Solomon said, "Wisdom." God rewarded such a discerning answer by giving him that wisdom as well as wealth and power. For many years Solomon lived a life that honored God.

Before it was all over, though, Solomon had slipped. He had gotten a little complacent. He had let some idolatry and some disillusionment slip into the royal household (along with the hundreds of wives and concubines). It was at this point that it is generally believed that he wrote the Book of Ecclesiastes.

For Every Season

You probably remember that famous passage: A time to "this" and a time to "that." Let's see how much of it you really remember. ...

There is a time for everything, and a season for every activity under heaven:

a time to be b____ and a time to die,

a time to plant and a time to up____,

a time to kill and a time to h___,

a time to tear down and a time to b____,

a time to w___ and a time to laugh,

a time to mourn and a time to d____,

a time to scatter stones and a time to g_____ them,

a time to e_____ and a time to refrain,

a time to search and a time to g___ up,

a time to keep and a time to t____ away,

a time to tear and a time to m____,

a time to be silent and a time to s_____,

a time to l____ and a time to hate,

a time for w___ and a time for peace. (Ecclesiastes 3:1–8)

Here Are the Answers

There is a time for everything, and a season for every activity under heaven:

a time to be born and a time to die,

a time to plant and a time to uproot,

a time to kill and a time to heal,

a time to tear down and a time to build,

a time to weep and a time to laugh,

a time to mourn and a time to dance,

a time to scatter stones and a time to gather them,

a time to embrace and a time to refrain,

a time to search and a time to give up,

a time to keep and a time to throw away,

a time to tear and a time to mend,

a time to be silent and a time to speak,

a time to love and a time to hate,

a time for war and a time for peace. (Ecclesiastes 3:1–8)

SCRIPTURE BITS

A phrase that is used umpteen times in Ecclesiastes is the phrase "under the sun." ("Umpteen" is a round figure depending on which translation you are using.) Another recurring theme is "everything is meaningless." Solomon should know; he had all the conveniences his culture offered him. And still, everything wasn't enough without God.

SONG OF SOLOMON

Here's the scoop. . .

Written: *around 950 B.C.*

Written by: *King Solomon*

Writing style: *a love poem*

One-liner: *I'm passionately in love, and I can't stop thinking about her. By Solomon.*

An Apple Fallen Not Far from the Tree

Solomon was the son of a musician and a soldier. His father, David, wrote many of the Psalms (which are poems or songs, remember). Solomon came from a creative bloodline. So, out of his love for a beautiful woman, one that he treasured, came this love poem that is inspired not by Cupid's arrow, but by God Himself.

THINK ABOUT IT THIS WAY

A PG-13 RATING?

It might not always seem like it at first glance, but the Bible is a very practical book. It deals with the issues of everyday life. The Song of Solomon is a good example. This is romantic love at its most syrupy and, sometimes, at its most seductive.

How the Theologians Feel

As you can imagine, this book of the Bible has created quite a stir through the centuries. For goodness' sake, parts of it are almost pillow talk (young Jewish boys were not allowed to read this book until they were thirteen years old). Because of that, many have been uncomfortable with the interpretation. After the dust has settled, most agree that Song of Solomon is a literal love poem about real people.

But also, most agree that this book is a great picture of how Christ feels about the church. The New Testament calls the church the "bride of Christ." In this way, the desire and passion that the king in this book shows for his bride is very akin to the desire and passion that Christ has toward us, His body, His church. We are valued. We are prized. We are an object of desire. We bring Him joy.

PROPHECY

The prophecies of the Old Testament include a lot of different kinds of information. They include stories (like in Daniel), wild visions (like in Ezekiel), sermons (like in Isaiah), and some future-telling. They are the writings of men who were plucked from their lives by God and were given a message. Their responsibility, then, was to get that message out. They came from a lot of different backgrounds. If you remember Jonah, then you remember that they were not all completely comfortable with God's call on their lives. But they all responded to it, and some of them quite creatively. Hosea was asked to marry a prostitute to show a picture of how God had loved an unfaithful Israel. Ezekiel gave part of his prophecy through pantomime (no record of white gloves or weird suspenders, though). Jeremiah wrote some of his message as funeral dirges.

Their writings are about as diverse as any collection you'll find. But they were the Billy Grahams of their day. They were the voices calling out to their country, "We're missing the point here! God wants to relate to us in a different way!" Because of that, their messages still have something to say to us today.

We have even greater confidence in the message proclaimed by the prophets. Pay close attention to what they wrote, for their words are like a light shining in a dark place—until the day Christ appears and His brilliant light shines in your hearts. Above all, you must understand that no prophecy in Scripture ever came from the prophets themselves or because they wanted to prophesy. It was the Holy Spirit who moved the prophets to speak from God. (2 Peter 1:19–21 NLT)

MAJOR PROPHETS	LESS MAJOR PROPHETS	
• Isaiah	• Hosea	• Nahum
• Jeremiah	• Joel	• Habakkuk
• Lamentations	• Amos	• Zephaniah
• Ezekiel	• Obadiah	• Haggai
• Daniel	• Jonah	• Zechariah
	• Micah	• Malachi

ISAIAH

Here's the scoop. . .

Written: *around 700 B.C.*

Written by: *Isaiah*

Writing style: *a collection of sermons and prophecies*

One-liner: *Pay attention. God has a master plan in the works and we need to be a part of it.*

A Prophet's Prophet

Isaiah preached to the Jewish people at a time when they didn't have much of a leg to stand on. They had refused to be faithful to God in worship. They had mixed and mingled their culture with the cultures of those around. They were a spear's throw from being taken to Babylon as exiles, thus completely losing hold of home.

How would you like to prepare a message for that crowd? What would you say? What Isaiah said was, essentially, "Let's examine the details of our lives, but let's find hope in the big picture. We might have messed things up royally, but God has a bigger plan to redeem the world. Let's hold onto that."

The First Part of Isaiah

The Book of Isaiah divides easily into two parts. The first thirty-nine chapters are about judgment. They refer to events current to Isaiah's day as well as events that haven't even happened yet today. You'll find that's true of much of the prophecy in the Bible. There was truth for the people then and there, but the prophecies also reflected a greater event in the more distant future.

God spoke through Isaiah with compassion and with an in-your-face-but-because-I-love-you kind of voice.

The Second Part

The last twenty-seven chapters of Isaiah (40–66) are often called the "Book of Consolation." They address Jesus' appearance in the New Testament. Isaiah 53 is one of the most famous and most picturesque prophecies about Jesus' birth, life, and death.

> *He was oppressed and he was afflicted, yet he never said a word. He was brought as a lamb to the slaughter; and as a sheep before her shearers is dumb, so he stood silent before the ones condemning him. From prison and trial they led him away to his death. But who among the people of that day realized it was their sins that he was dying for—that he was suffering their punishment? He was buried like a criminal in a rich man's grave; but he had done no wrong, and had never spoken an evil word.*
> *(Isaiah 53:7–9 TLB)*

No one knew better than Isaiah that when Christ came to earth He would suffer greatly so that we would not have to.

Isaiah Put to Music?

Have you ever heard Handel's *Messiah?* It's a classical choral piece performed often around Christmas. The most well-known song from the collection is the "Hallelujah Chorus," which has appeared in everything from church sanctuaries to sitcoms and commercials.

Anyway, if you've heard Handel's *Messiah,* you've heard parts of Isaiah put to music. Check out these Scripture lyrics and see if they ring a bell or two. The Scriptures listed below are from the *King James Version* of the Bible, which uses an older style of English. It is the version Handel quoted.

"Every valley shall be exalted, and every mountain and hill shall be made low: and the crooked shall be made straight, and the rough places plain" (Isaiah 40:4). *This describes God's truth revealed in Jesus Christ.*

"For unto us a child is born, unto us a son is given: and the government shall be upon his shoulder: and his name shall be called Wonderful, Counsellor, The mighty God, The everlasting Father, the Prince of Peace" (Isaiah 9:6). *So many songs have been based on this verse in one version or another.*

"He is despised and rejected of men; a man of sorrows, and acquainted with grief: and we hid as it were our faces from him; he was despised, and we esteemed him not" (Isaiah 53:3). *Jesus was not accepted among his peers. He wasn't recognized for who He was.*

"But he was wounded for our transgressions, he was bruised for our iniquities: the chastisement of our peace was upon him; and with his stripes we are healed" (Isaiah 53:5). *Jesus died for our sins. The stripes refer to the flogging He received before He was killed.*

"All we like sheep have gone astray; we have turned every one to his own way; and the Lord hath laid on him the iniquity of us all" (Isaiah 53:6). *This is the bottom line of the gospel: Jesus sacrificed Himself for our sin (that's what iniquity is).*

JEREMIAH

IN CONTEXT

Here's the scoop. . .

Written: *around 600 B.C.*

Written by: *Jeremiah*

Writing style: *a prophecy or message from God*

One-liner: *Prepare to face the consequences of living apart from God. Know that God's plan is still in place, though.*

Weeping and Wailing

Jeremiah had a life that few of us would wish for. He experienced a lot of rejection. He spent most of his whole life and certainly all of his adult life grieving for the mistakes of his fellow citizens. He was a prophet who didn't get a lot of glory.

Jeremiah preached mostly in Judah, the southern kingdom of Israel. Like all of Israel, these people had drifted farther and farther from God's way of doing things. At first Jeremiah's prophecies were warnings such as, "You know what ALWAYS happens when we don't follow God. We get weaker and weaker until some other country takes us over. It's about to happen again."

Later in his ministry, his prophecies resembled something more like, "Well, you've made your bed now. You need to get ready to lie in it. You've become too weak with sin and idolatry to fight off any enemy at all. Accept that something bad is going to happen."

Still later he gave up on trying to amend the current situation and instead began to prophesy about the long-term salvation that was ahead of them. His message was, "We have wasted this time as a nation. But there is always eventual hope because God promised a Messiah who will fix this mess we've created."

Sure enough, Jeremiah's people did become captives in Babylonia. Sure enough, about six hundred years later, Jesus did come to give them, and us, hope.

LAMENTATIONS

Here's the scoop. . .

Written: *around 600 B.C.*

Written by: *Jeremiah*

Writing style: *sermons or prophecies in the form of funeral dirges*

One-liner: *What we dreaded has happened. Our sin has destroyed us. My heart is broken.*

Nobody Likes Me, Everybody Hates Me, Think I'll Eat Some Worms. . .

Think of the saddest song you know and you'll be in the right mood for reading Lamentations. The Book of Lamentations is actually five Hebrew poems. They are so sad that they are considered funeral dirges. Chapters 1 through 4 are actually acrostics in Hebrews—you know, where the first letter of each line spells something. In the case of these chapters, the first letters of each line are the letters of the Hebrew alphabet. (For Chapter 3 it's every three verses.) Chapter 5 is the only chapter that is not alphabetical, but it is still a poem.

We spend so much of our lives not worrying about sin that it's hard to understand Jeremiah's getting so worked up about it. Actually, the people of his day felt the same way. They ridiculed Jeremiah. They rejected his message. But that didn't change the fact that what he said came true. He had told them that if they didn't straighten up, they would lose their land again and…guess what? Sure enough, they were taken captive into Babylonia.

As far as we know, Lamentations was written for the people while they were captives. It was pretty good of Jeremiah, when you think about it, to warn the people, be disregarded by them, then to write them some sad songs when they needed them. (Sad songs say so much, you know.)

Lamentations could have been a told-you-so book. Jeremiah had, indeed, warned the people about the consequences of their sin. But, rather than being a told-you-so book, Jeremiah is a book of sadness that his people were separated once again from their land and disobedient to God, which caused them to be separated from their land.

EZEKIEL

IN CONTEXT

Here's the scoop. . .

Written: *around 550 B.C.*

Written by: *Ezekiel*

Writing style: *a sermon or prophecy*

One-liner: *I saw some visions from God's perspective on how we've lived our lives and of heaven. Let me describe them.*

A Man with a Vision

That's Ezekiel. Not just one vision, either. Many visions. The Book of Ezekiel is a colorful prophecy. It includes judgment and condemnation. It's almost kicking the people while they are down, since he was preaching to them while they were exiled from their homes. The book also includes visions of heaven and hope for the future.

Because Ezekiel is such an imaginative book, it can seem difficult to wade through at times. Just remember this is the writing of a man to whom God is showing spectacular things. Ezekiel is trying to describe his visions of heaven and of heavenly things in human terms. Basically, that is impossible. So he says a lot of "It was like. . ." kind of statements. In the end we'll all have to wait until we see God to really understand what Ezekiel saw.

A Vision of God

Sometimes, just as a cute adult thing to do, we ask little kids what they think God looks like. Some responses are hilarious, but none are ever like Ezekiel's view of God. Listen to this:

> For high in the sky above them was what looked like a throne made of beautiful blue sapphire stones, and upon it sat someone who appeared to be a Man. From his waist up, he seemed to be all glowing bronze, dazzling like fire; and from his waist down he seemed to be entirely flame, and there was

a glowing halo like a rainbow all around him. That was the way the glory of the Lord appeared to me. And when I saw it, I fell face downward on the ground. (Ezekiel 1:26–28 TLB)

And listen to his description of the angels around God's throne:

- Their form was that of a man. . . each of them had four faces and four wings.

- Their legs were straight; their feet were like those of a calf and gleamed like burnished bronze.

- Under their wings they had the hands of a man.

- Each of the four had the face of a man. . .the face of a lion. . .the face of an ox. . .also the face of an eagle.

- The appearance of the living creatures was like burning coals of fire or like torches. . . . The creatures sped back and forth like flashes of lightning.

- I saw a wheel on the ground beside each creature with its four faces. . . . Their rims were high and awesome, and all four rims were full of eyes all around. (See Ezekiel 1:5–21.)

The Holy Mime

Ezekiel actually acted out part of his prophecy much like a mime would. He went for a long time without speaking. He went for an even longer time lying in exactly the same place. He went to some great lengths to get his point across.

THINK ABOUT IT THIS WAY

Whether we understand Ezekiel's vision or not, we can understand his message that there is reality beyond what we can see and there is hope beyond any difficulty we might face.

Which Bones?

One of the most powerful images of Ezekiel is the valley of dry bones. The bones represented Israel, with no hope. God breathed life into the bones to show Ezekiel that there was hope for Israel and that they would one day return to their land. Do you recognize that story? You might recognize it more this way:

> Dem bones, Dem bones, Dem dry bones,
> Dem bones, Dem bones, Dem dry bones,
> Dem bones, Dem bones, Dem dry bones,
> Now hear the word of the Lord.

The toe bone connected to the ankle bone, the ankle bone connected to the leg bone, the leg bone connected to the hip bone, etcetera, etcetera, etcetera. . . . (See Ezekiel 37:1–14.)

DANIEL

IN CONTEXT

Here's the scoop. . .

Written: *around 550 B.C.*

Written by: *Daniel*

Writing style: *some stories and some visions and some prophecies*

One-liner: *Here are the stories of Daniel, a Jewish exile in Babylonia, and his visions of the future.*

Daniel: The Story

The first six chapters of the Book of Daniel tell his story. It's like a mini-series set in the midst of the exile of the Jewish people. Daniel was a young adult when his people were taken captive into Babylonia.

First, the Babylonians tried to feed him rich foods that were taboo for a young Jewish boy. He opted for vegetables and fruits. Before you knew it, he had influenced the guards to serve all the boys healthier meals.

Next, he became a servant to the king and even interpreted the king's dreams. Because of this, he was put in charge of all the wise men in Babylonia.

As you can imagine, this did not set well with the Babylonian locals. They set a trap, convincing the king to give an order for everyone, including the Jewish people, to bow down to an idol. Daniel and his friends refused. You've probably heard the miraculous story of the three friends' being thrown into the fiery furnace (a form of capital punishment) and not only surviving, but not even smelling of smoke.

In another attempt to trip Daniel up, a decree was sent out that no one could pray to God for thirty days. Daniel, of course, continued to pray. His punishment was to be thrown into a cave with hungry lions. Believe it or not, not one lion touched Daniel.

Daniel: The Prophecy

The last half of the Book of Daniel is made up of Daniel's prophecies. As far as we know, many of those prophecies have already been fulfilled. Some, though, refer to the same time period as described in the Book of Revelation (New Testament), the end of the world.

HOSEA

Here's the scoop. . .

Written: *around 700 B.C.*

Written by: *Hosea*

Writing style: *a collection of Hosea's prophecies mixed in with stories about his life*

One-liner: *Ephraim, you are as unfaithful to God as a prostitute to her husband. Turn around.*

The Big "Huh?"

If anybody knows anything about Hosea, it is usually that he was the prophet who married the prostitute. Huh?

Why? Because God told him to.

Why would God tell him to do that? So that his life could be a picture of how much God loved Israel whether they loved Him back or not.

Why would God compare Israel to a prostitute? Good question. The answer to that question is the foundation for understanding the prophecy of Hosea. The collective Hebrew people were very much like a prostitute because they were unfaithful to God. God had asked them to worship only Him, no idols, no false gods—a monogamous worship relationship. Sometimes the people would obey God, usually when they needed God's help. But, as soon as they were doing okay, they forgot their allegiance and began to worship whatever was the popular idol of the day.

This had been going on for years. It had weakened them politically. It had caused them to lose their homes, their battles, their well-being. It was about to cause them to be taken captive to another land as exiles. That's why God asked Hosea to go to such desperate lengths. Basically God said, "Marry a call-girl and let her despicable actions toward you show these people how they have treated me." In other words, Hosea's marriage was another of God's object lessons.

Hosea did it. He married a prostitute. They had three children together. Hosea's wife, Gomer (go figure), constantly broke Hosea's heart by going back to her old life, no matter how much he loved her or how well he treated her.

A Message to Ephraim

The prophecy of Hosea isn't just a story of his marriage, though. Hosea was a prophet in the northern kingdom of Israel. He addressed his message to the tribe of Ephraim, the largest tribe of that kingdom, but it was a message for all Hebrews. He called their hand on several issues: the instability of their commitment to God, their diluted identity as followers of God, and their spiritual superficiality.

Maybe some of the Israelites listened. We don't know. They didn't repent of their religious prostitution. They kept right on worshiping other gods until they were destroyed as a nation.

JOEL

Here's the scoop. . .

Written: *around 800* B.C.

Written by: *Joel, a prophet to Judah, the southern kingdom*

Writing style: *a collection of sermons*

One-liner: *Because of our sin, it's going to get worse before it gets better. But it will get better one day.*

Grasshoppers on the Loose

In the Old Testament God's judgment for sin came in the form of many things. In the plagues of Egypt, God's judgment came in the form of death and bugs and sickness and weather.

The Book of Joel is a red-flag message to the people of Judah that God had just about had enough of their waywardness and rebellion. Joel was specific, as well. He told his people that their punishment would come in the form of locusts—flying, grasshopper-like bugs that fed off the vegetation of the land.

Punishment by grasshoppers might not sound like much more to us than an inconvenience and a great time to stock up on bug repellant. We need to understand the culture of that day, though. People lived off the land. They farmed; they raised food for their animals. If a huge swarm of locusts came through and destroyed all the vegetation, the people would have nothing. The livestock would die. Everyone would eventually starve.

(Even worse, some people believe that Joel was using locusts as an illustration of Assyrian soldiers rushing to take over Judah. There was no Assyrian soldier repellant.)

When Joel gave this gloom-and-doom prophecy, everything was going pretty well in Judah. It was difficult for the people to think of hard times when they had plenty to eat. That's probably why they didn't listen to Joel. When life is easy, it's not hard to disregard God's warning that sin destroys.

And in the Future...

Joel did give a little good news as well. Like many other prophets, his message included an in-the-future clause. He not only predicted Judah's destruction because of their sin, but also Judah's eventual salvation through God's eventual forgiveness.

People today refer to prophecies of Joel as well when they discuss the end of the world as we know it. There's a lot of vision packed in this three-chapter manuscript.

SCRIPTURE BITS

Joel's words appear not only here in his prophecy, but also in the New Testament. You might remember that at the beginning of Acts, God comes to the church in a new way—as the Holy Spirit. It's a wild time of multi-languages and fire from heaven. In the midst of it all, Peter quotes Joel. Here's part of what Peter said:

"What you see this morning was predicted centuries ago by the prophet Joel—'In the last days,' God said, 'I will pour out my Holy Spirit upon all mankind, and your sons and daughters shall prophesy, and your young men shall see visions, and your old men dream dreams. Yes, the Holy Spirit shall come upon all my servants, men and women alike, and they shall prophesy.'"

Acts 2:16–18 TLB

AMOS

IN CONTEXT

Here's the scoop. . .

Written: *around 750 B.C.*

Written by: *Amos, a prophet from Judah (southern kingdom) who preached to Israel (northern kingdom)*

Writing style: *a sermon or prophecy*

One-liner: *By human standards, you're measuring up, but by God's standards you're failing.*

A Lesson in Irony

Amos was a fish out of water in a lot of ways. He was from the southern kingdom, but he preached to the northern kingdom. He was a shepherd, but he preached to rich people. His message was somewhat negative, but he was preaching to people who were having a great time.

The meat of Amos's message was that God was not satisfied with the worship of His people in Israel. They were coming to the temple to worship, then making their living by exploiting the poor of their society. They were doing some of the right ceremonial things, but they weren't worshiping God with the way they lived their lives. For this, God, through Amos, condemned them.

One of the ways in which God directed Amos to warn the people was through an object lesson. God showed Amos a plumb line. A plumb line was a string with a weight that showed a workman whether his work was straight. It was like a vertical level. God told Amos that He was holding a plumb line up to Israel to see if their ways were straight or not. They were definitely not making the grade compared to God's plumb line.

OBADIAH

IN CONTEXT

Here's the scoop. . .

Written: *around 850 B.C.*

Written by: *Obadiah*

Writing style: *an announcement of judgment*

One-liner: *Attention, people of Edom: You've bullied Israel and now you'll answer to God.*

You'll Get Yours

Obadiah is unique in that he didn't preach to Israel or Judah. Instead he preached on their behalf to the Edomites.

A little background: Many generations before, the country of Edom originated from a man named Esau, whose name later became Edom. Esau was the twin brother to Jacob, whose name was later changed to Israel. In other words, the Israelites and the Edomites descended from twin brothers. Just as Esau and Jacob had their differences (Genesis 25–27), the Israelites and the Edomites had theirs.

Obadiah's prophecy is basically a condemnation of Edom for NOT helping Israel defend itself and for being a bully to Israel. Obadiah prophesied that the whole nation of Edom would eventually die out. By A.D. 70, they had.

Talk About a Soap Opera

The actual skinny about the Edomites and the Israelites reads like a daytime drama.

Esau (later named Edom) and Jacob (later named Israel) were twin boys who, even in the womb, fought to see who would be the better, the first. Esau was born first, which meant he had the family birthright. This birthright became a conflict that lasted their whole lives.

Esau was a rough outdoorsman. Jacob was just the opposite. One day Esau came in from hunting and he was ravenously hungry. Jacob talked him into trading his birthright for some stew. Yes, you read it right. Birthright for stew.

THINK ABOUT IT THIS WAY

You might ask yourself, why is somebody else's "hate" mail a part of the Bible? Obadiah's message is like a coin with two sides. One side is a very fiery denunciation of Edom. But the other side of the coin is a look into the "momma bear" side of God's attitude toward His people. Obadiah reveals to us a side of God that does not sit back and leave us to our enemies undefended. Obadiah's message says that when God steps in, He will have the final word. The one who defends us has the power to get the job done.

The birthright was really nothing without the blessing of their dad (Isaac) to go along with it. When the time came, Jacob dressed up like Esau and went to his dad in disguise to receive Esau's blessing. Isaac was old and almost blind. He mistakenly promised Jacob the bigger part of the inheritance and the leadership role in the family. That might not sound binding today, but in that day it meant everything.

When Esau got back to the house that day, he realized that he had been snookered out of his future as a leader and a rich man. He was left to make his home among foreigners. This is why he ended up in Edom with a huge grudge that he passed down through generations.

Talk about family feud.

JONAH

IN CONTEXT

Here's the scoop. . .

Written: *around 750 B.C.*

Written by: *Jonah*

Writing style: *the story of Jonah's prophecy to Nineveh*

One-liner: *Jonah unwillingly prophesies to a wicked place and is disappointed at the good turnout.*

A Fishy Story

The story of Jonah is a classic story of My Way vs. God's Way. God told Jonah to go to Nineveh and prophesy. Jonah headed the opposite direction. At first this can seem like a very rebellious thing for Jonah to do. Was he just disobedient? Did he not want to serve God?

Like most human dilemmas it's more complicated than that. Do you know where Nineveh was? Nineveh was the capital of the country that was the biggest enemy of Jonah's country. To prophesy to Nineveh, Jonah had to violate every racial and political prejudice that was a part of his fabric. He wanted God to judge Nineveh for their cruelty rather than give them an opportunity to repent. Most of us would have felt the same way if we had stood in Jonah's sandals.

Back to the story, Jonah got the call from God and jumped on a boat headed in the opposite direction. The boat ran into a storm, and a bad storm at that. Destruction was soon at hand when the sailors realized that God was after something. Jonah "fessed up" and they (*splash!*) threw him overboard. Jonah was swallowed by a big fish and had three days in a dark, briny belly to contemplate his next move.

Jonah did some praying while he was in the fish, and after those three days, the fish regurgitated him (yuck!) on the beach. God once again said to go to Nineveh; Jonah went.

Thus far this story is pretty familiar. The belly-of-the-fish part is the famous part. But there is more.

When Jonah got to Nineveh, he preached to the people and, evil as they were, they responded graciously. They repented of their sin and banned evil from their city.

How did Jonah respond, this great prophet of God?

He was disappointed. He had gone to a lot of trouble and come a long way and here these people had changed their ways and gotten off the hook. Jonah sat himself down and had a big ol' pity party.

Then God did one of those object lessons that leaves us going, "huh?" One day a plant grew up around Jonah that kept him in the shade. This was a great thing. But the next day, a worm killed the plant, leaving Jonah back in the sun.

Jonah complained to God. Now, get the picture. Here is a man who spent three days in the belly of a fish and he's complaining because a worm ate a vine. God gave Jonah a little talking-to.

 THINK ABOUT IT THIS WAY

So, this is the question: What is the story of Jonah really about? Is it about a wicked town called Nineveh getting a second chance? Is it about a thick-headed prophet who needed to learn some lessons? Is it about a God who wants everyone to leave their self-destructive ways, no matter what they've done or who they are? Is it about a God-follower who would rather see the bad guys get theirs (their just desserts, not their gracious forgiveness) than God get His? We can all find ourselves in a lot of different roles in this story. It's worth reviewing.

MICAH

IN CONTEXT

Here's the scoop. . .

Written: *around 600 B.C.*

Written by: *Micah*

Writing style: *several sermons based on visions from God*

One-liner: *We are immoral at every level and headed for destruction. Only God can deliver us from ourselves.*

Good News, Bad News

The prophet Micah was unique in that he preached or prophesied to both the northern kingdom of Israel (called Samaria) and to the southern kingdom of Judah. The other prophets preached to either one or the other. But, like the other prophets, he did prophesy both good news and bad news. He prophesied of judgment that was coming to the Hebrews and of the future victory that would come through Jesus Christ.

Micah was a down-to-earth prophet who looked around himself and saw a mess. He didn't mince words whether he was describing the evil he saw, the destruction that was coming, or the hope of the future. He called his people back to a heart devotion instead of a faith that just goes through the motions. He foretold their exile from their homes, which did eventually happen. He also foretold the actual place of Christ's birth, Bethlehem.

> ### SCRIPTURE BITS
>
> *Micah had a way of cutting to the chase.*
>
> **He has told you what he wants, and this is all it is: to be fair and just and merciful, and to walk humbly with your God.**
>
> ***Micah 6:8*** TLB

NAHUM

IN CONTEXT

Here's the scoop. . .

Written: *around 650 B.C.*

Written by: *Nahum*

Writing style: *a sermon*

One-liner: *No matter how strong evil seems, God will do away with it when He is ready.*

Who Is God?

Nahum was a prophet in Judah. His prophecy was written in a form of poetry. It opened with some strong statements about God's power and goodness. Nahum established God's power to take care of His own. Then when Nahum had made his point, he turned his attention to a force of evil in his day and time—Nineveh.

What Is Nineveh?

Assyria was Israel and Judah's neighbor to the east, and Assyria was a bully of a neighbor. First Assyria took over Israel. Once that happened, Judah and its capital, Jerusalem, were under constant threat. Nahum directed his prophecy to Assyria and particularly to its capital, Nineveh.

Remember that Nineveh was the town that Jonah prophesied to after the whole big-fish-regurgitating-a-prophet-on-the-beach fiasco. One of the reasons Jonah hadn't wanted to preach to Nineveh was that they were the enemy. That was also why he was less than thrilled when they repented and God did not destroy them. That was about one hundred years before Nahum's day.

Nineveh did not stay in a repented state. They returned to their evil ways. Nahum faced them with the news that God would punish their evil once and for all. Hands down. No holds barred. Sparing no expense. No questions asked.

HABAKKUK

IN CONTEXT

Here's the scoop. . .

Written: *around 600 B.C.*

Written by: *Habakkuk*

Writing style: *a sermon in the form of questions and answers*

One-liner: *God, why don't You stop bad things from happening?*

The Hard Questions

Habakkuk was honest enough to ask the hard questions. In fact, that was how his prophecy began. As refreshing as it is to hear a prophet of God ask the questions we have often asked, it's even more refreshing to know that Habakkuk got answers.

Basically, God told Habakkuk what a lot of good dads tell their kids: You're going to have to trust Me to take care of this in My own time. God said that punishing evil was up to Him, alone. He reminded Habakkuk, though, that evil would not go unpunished, in the end.

One of the interesting things about Habakkuk's prophecy is that he began with hard questions, but he ended with worship. That happens a lot when you sit with God long enough to hear His answers and to trust them. After Habakkuk listened to God, he accepted God's control over the situation. He closed with this prayer:

> *Though the fig tree does not bud and there are no grapes on the vines,*
> *though the olive crop fails and the fields produce no food,*
> *though there are no sheep in the pen and no cattle in the stalls. . .*

(In Habakkuk's day this meant, "though the economy is going to pot and we aren't going to survive.")

> *yet I will rejoice in the LORD, I will be joyful in God my Savior.*
> *(Habakkuk 3:17–18)*

Most of us define who God is in our lives according to our current circumstances. Habakkuk looked into the face of the worst of life and still found there God's faithfulness.

SCRIPTURE BITS

Habakkuk asks God the kinds of questions we would often like to ask:

How long, O LORD, must I call for help, but you do not listen?

Or cry out to you, "Violence!" but you do not save?

Why do you make me look at injustice?

Why do you tolerate wrong?

Habakkuk 1:2–3

Comparison

Habakkuk was a lot like David in the fact that he was willing to look through the "hard stuff" to see God. Compare this writing of David to that of Habakkuk.

But as for me, I came so close to the edge of the cliff! My feet were slipping, and I was almost gone. For I envied the proud when I saw them prosper despite their wickedness. They seem to live such a painless life; their bodies are so healthy and strong. They aren't troubled like other people or plagued with problems like everyone else.

And so the people are dismayed and confused, drinking in all their words. "Does God realize what is going on?" they ask. "Is the Most High even aware of what is happening?"

Then I realized how bitter I had become, how pained I had been by all I had seen. I was so foolish and ignorant—I must have seemed like a senseless animal to you. Yet I still belong to you; you are holding my right hand. You will keep on guiding me with your counsel, leading me to a glorious destiny. Whom have I in heaven but you? I desire you more than anything on earth. My health may fail, and my spirit may grow weak, but God remains the strength of my heart; he is mine forever. (Psalm 73:2–5, 10–11, 21–26 NLT)

ZEPHANIAH

IN CONTEXT

Here's the scoop. . .

Written: *around 630* B.C.

Written by: *Zephaniah*

Writing style: *a message directly from God*

One-liner: *God will hold us accountable for our actions. All of them.*

Zephaniah was one of the last prophets to Judah before they were taken captive into Babylonia. His message, though first to Judah, was to all nations. He reminded the Hebrews that God would hold them accountable for their actions. He reminds us still today.

The first section of Zephaniah, which is the section on judgment, is classic among the prophets. You may have heard the term "hellfire and brimstone" to describe a preacher who is really letting his listeners have it. Zephaniah's message started out that way. Then, gradually he moved from a place of condemnation to a place of hope.

Zephaniah actually followed the pattern of many self-help groups today. First, he knew the people needed to recognize just how much they had messed up. Then he could offer them hope that they weren't alone in their situation. The last portion of Zephaniah even points to the coming of Christ as the greatest hope of salvation.

HAGGAI

Here's the scoop. . .

Written: *around 500 B.C.*

Written by: *Haggai*

Writing style: *five short sermons*

One-liner: *Don't ignore what matters most—your relationship with your God and Creator!*

Setting Priorities

The book of Haggai is about priorities. Unlike the Book of Zephaniah, written before the exile from Judah to Babylon, Haggai is written after the exile. The people have returned to Judah, but are putting off making God a priority by restoring their place of worship, the temple. Haggai basically confronts them with their procrastination: What are you doing leaving God's house in a mess so you can work on your own?

Haggai's message can seem a little backward to us. After all, we are always hearing that expression, "Charity starts at home." Weren't the people right to work on their own homes first? Well. . .remember two things:

1. *It had been at least ten years since they returned home.* It's not like Haggai was telling them to rebuild the temple before they even unpacked their bags. They had established a pattern of not getting around to it.

2. *The problem all along with the Jewish people, in fact the reason they lost their homes to begin with, was a lack of priority on worship.* God had told them, "Only worship me." But they hadn't listened. Rebuilding the temple would be a significant step to establishing a new pattern of living. It was about their own attention to their spiritual well-being, not just a building.

Haggai also spoke to the people about the future temple. That meant way in the future, when Jesus would return to earth and the new heaven and new earth would be in place. Coming from Haggai, this served as a reminder that better days were ahead.

ZECHARIAH

IN CONTEXT

Here's the scoop. . .

Written: *around 500* B.C.

Written by: *Zechariah*

Writing style: *two sermons*

One-liner: *Finish the temple and get your relationship with God in working order. The Messiah is coming!!*

It's About Time!

The first part of the Book of Zechariah relates most closely to the rebuilding of the temple in Jerusalem. Zechariah wrote to motivate the people. "It really is worth it!" was Zechariah's message.

The second part of Zechariah holds more prophecies about Jesus than any other Old Testament prophet.

- Jesus rode into Jerusalem riding on a donkey a week before He died (Zechariah 9:9).

- Judas betrayed Jesus Christ for thirty pieces of silver (Zechariah 11:12).

- Jesus' side was pierced during the crucifixion (Zechariah 12:10).

- Jesus' blood cleansed our sin (Zechariah 13:1).

- Jesus had scars in His hands and side (Zechariah 13:6).

- Jesus was arrested and deserted by His disciples (Zechariah 13:7).

- Zechariah also prophesied Jesus' second return to reign on earth (Zechariah 14:4; Revelation 11:15).

MALACHI

IN CONTEXT

Here's the scoop. . .

Written: *around 400 B.C.*

Written by: *Malachi*

Writing style: *a sermon in the form of questions and answers*

One-liner: *Worshiping God is not about doing the least to get by. Be wholehearted instead.*

Last, But Not Least

Malachi is the prophet who connects the Old Testament to the New Testament. He prophesied about John the Baptist and he was the last prophet until John the Baptist. While not all the books of the Old Testament are in chronological order, Malachi really is. It was the last book written and it is the last book in the Old Testament.

Malachi reminded the people that they were making a halfhearted attempt at keeping God's law. They brought their sacrifices, but they brought the most damaged of their animals and crops. They were living as if God could not see their hearts and know that they didn't really honor Him. They were doing the least they could to still have some semblance of a life of faith.

Malachi also reprimanded the people for the same practice that the Hebrews were guilty of since they came to their land: They continued to marry into families who worshiped idols and so the Hebrews would begin to mix idol worship into their own worship. In Malachi's day, the men were even divorcing their Hebrew wives to marry foreign wives.

Malachi foretold the coming of John the Baptist as well as Jesus Christ.

NEW TESTAMENT BOOK SUMMARIES

T he following pages include a little information about each of the books in the New Testament. Just like with the Old Testament, these books are marked off in sections (Gospels, history, letters, prophecy), but they are in the order that they appear in the Bible.

For each book you can read some facts and a one-liner overview, or you can dig a little deeper and read over the major stories or points of that book.

Keep in mind that this was a phenomenal time in world history as well as Christian history. The life of Christ changed everything—power structures, world views, etc. You know how you feel when you are working on a new project that is really important to you? Maybe you're working on a project like building a house through Habitat for Humanity or helping at the homeless shelter. Think of setting out on a project that you really believe in. That is the kind of atmosphere in which these books were written, but it was LIFE for these guys rather than a weeklong excursion.

Get a load of this accusation made against the early Christian leaders:

> But the Jewish leaders were jealous, so they gathered some worthless fellows from the streets to form a mob and start a riot. They attacked the home of Jason, searching for Paul and Silas so they could drag them out to the crowd. Not finding them there, they dragged out Jason and some of the other believers instead and took them before the city council. "Paul and Silas have turned the rest of the world upside down, and now they are here disturbing our city," they shouted. (Acts 17:5–6 NLT)

Turning the world upside down. That's what the New Testament is really about.

THE GOSPELS

There are four Gospels. They are each written by a different person. You've probably heard them called, "the Gospel according to Matthew," "the Gospel according to Mark," and so on. "Gospel" means "good news." The good news was that Jesus was the Messiah. Each of these men wanted to write about Jesus' life in such a way that he could convince his audience that Jesus really was the one that God had promised throughout history.

The Gospels aren't really biographies in that the authors don't each try to write down Jesus' life in chronological order. They each organized what they wanted to say differently. They included different information. Matthew was writing to a Jewish audience so he included a lot of quotes from the Old Testament. Mark was writing to a Roman (or non-Jewish) audience so he didn't refer back to Jewish history in any big way at all. Each writer brought a different slant to the story. What they had in common, though, was that they desperately wanted their readers to understand that Jesus wasn't just one more martyr, just one more prophet, just one more Christian celebrity. Instead, Jesus was the Messiah that the whole Old Testament had wrapped its hope around. Jesus was the fulfillment of God's promise to make an open door between Himself and humanity. Jesus was God coming to us to pay the price for humanity's waywardness.

IN CONTEXT

The Gospels

- Matthew

- Mark

- Luke

- John

MATTHEW

Here's the scoop. . .

Written: *around* A.D. 60

Written by: *Matthew*

Writing style: *a biographical narrative, a collection of true stories*

One-liner: *Hebrew friends, Jesus is the Messiah that God promised through the prophets, and here's how I know.*

Matthew's Take on It

This was Matthew's slant: Jesus is the promised Messiah. Matthew included more Old Testament prophecies than any other writer. He traced Jesus' genealogy back to Abraham, who is the father of the Hebrews. Matthew established Jesus' role as the one that his people had been waiting for.

The Book of Matthew is the first of four Gospels, or versions of the story of Christ. Each of the Gospels has a different slant, a different perspective. They tell the stories in a different order or with different details. Each of the writers gives a true, but different viewpoint on Jesus' life.

The Problem

Unfortunately, that was pretty difficult for the Hebrews to swallow. Throughout the Old Testament, they had heard the promise of the Messiah. Each time they were oppressed (even if it was a consequence of their own sin), they comforted themselves by remembering the promise of the Messiah. The problem was, they thought the Messiah was going to be a political and military ruler who would destroy their enemies with a single blast. That was not the kind of Messiah Jesus was, at least not this first time around.

As Matthew revealed, Jesus came to die for our sins, not beat up our enemies. He came to show us another way of *living,* not winning. He came to save us from ourselves.

This is why the religious leaders of the day didn't get it. Here was the Jesus they had watched grow up. They knew His parents. They had been to His hometown. He didn't look like anything special to them. And He was claiming to be God?!? They just couldn't go for that. Add to that the fact that Jesus confronted them on a regular basis about their own hypocrisy, and they were first upset, then resentful, then jealous, then out to get Him.

So after all the dust had settled, after Jesus had lived before Matthew's eyes and worked miracles and died, had come back to life and gone back to heaven, then Matthew sat down to set the record straight. He methodically recorded the events and the teachings of Jesus' life so that (in his mind) any reader would know, without a doubt, that Jesus was the Messiah.

A New Kingdom

Jesus had come to establish a new kingdom all right, it just wasn't the kingdom of Israel. It was a new kingdom in people's hearts. That was a difficult concept to understand. It was easier to reject Jesus and look for someone else who fit the expectations a little better.

Matthew closed his version of Jesus' life with a famous statement that we now call the "Great Commission."

> *"Therefore go and make disciples of all nations, baptizing them in the name of the Father and of the Son and of the Holy Spirit, and teaching them to obey everything I have commanded you. And surely I am with you always, to the very end of the age." (Matthew 28:19–20)*

In other words, Jesus came to establish the kingdom of heaven in the hearts of people. Then He wanted His followers to go and do the same.

SCRIPTURE BITS

The Be-A-Ti-Whats?

The Beatitudes are probably the most famous passage in Matthew. How's your memory?

Blessed are the poor in spirit, for theirs is the . . .
Blessed are those who mourn, for they will be . . .
Blessed are the meek, for they will inherit the . . .
Blessed are those who hunger and thirst for righteousness, for they will be . . .
Blessed are the merciful, for they will be shown . . .
Blessed are the pure in heart, for they will see . . .
Blessed are the peacemakers, for they will be called sons of . . .
Blessed are those who are persecuted because of their righteousness, for theirs is the kingdom of . . .

Matthew 5:3–10

Answer Key

kingdom of heaven
comforted
earth
filled
mercy
God
God
heaven

MARK

Here's the scoop. . .

Written: *around* A.D. 60

Written by: *John Mark*

Writing style: *a biographical narrative*

One-liner: *Hey Romans, Jesus was a servant-king.*
Look what He did!

Lights, ACTION!!

Mark was a writer who loved action verbs. He wrote about what Christ did, His miracles especially. Mark's Gospel is the shortest of all four Gospels. It is the most "to the point."

Mark represented Jesus as a servant. He displayed Jesus' miracles as acts of compassion. Almost half of the Book of Mark covers the last eight days of Jesus' life where He gave Himself away for our salvation—His greatest act of servanthood.

Mark and Matthew wrote from different standpoints. Matthew focused on the Messiah-ship of Jesus. Mark focused on the servant leadership of Jesus. Matthew spoke to a Jewish audience and built his case based on Jewish tradition. Mark spoke to a Roman audience and focused on Jesus' compassion for all humanity. Mark told three miracles of Jesus in the first chapter, where Matthew only had one miracle in the first seven chapters. Matthew opened with the birth of Christ, but Mark opened with Jesus as an adult.

Mark's Sources

Though Mark was not a disciple of Jesus, he was connected to Jesus in several ways. The disciples met at his mother's home. He was very close to the disciple Peter. His cousin was Barnabas, a colleague of the apostle Paul. Mark even traveled with Paul and Barnabas for a time on one of their missionary journeys.

Since Mark was a "cut-to-the-chase" kind of guy he had some real bottom-line verses that put a lot of truth in a little space for us to digest:

> Then [Jesus] called the crowd to him along with his disciples and said: "If anyone would come after me, he must deny himself and take up his cross and follow me. For whoever wants to save his life will lose it, but whoever loses his life for me and for the gospel will save it. What good is it for a man to gain the whole world, yet forfeit his soul?" (Mark 8:34–36)

> "For even the Son of Man did not come to be served, but to serve, and to give his life as a ransom for many." (Mark 10:45)

Mark's Gospel was such an action-packed, bottom-line kind of description of Jesus' life and work that Matthew and Luke used Mark's work as a source for their own Gospels.

The Last Week of Jesus' Ministry

Of the sixteen chapters in Mark, the last seven (almost half!) covered the last week of Christ's life. Chapter 11 opened with Jesus' entry into Jerusalem. This event was perhaps the most misunderstood event of Christ's adult ministry. The people were looking for a king, a political military leader who could rid them of their oppression. When they welcomed Jesus that day into the city, they thought they were welcoming that kind of leader.

But Jesus was coming to Jerusalem to die for the sins of the world, not to become a national leader for a small nation.

Mark recorded several significant events from that last week of Jesus' life to help his readers understand Jesus' mission. He recorded conversations that Jesus had with the religious leaders of the day, trying to clarify for them that He was the Son of God. But all they could ask Him about were taxes and trick questions in a feeble attempt to prove their superiority.

Mark also recorded the story you've probably heard about the widow who gave her small offering—two coins. Jesus used her offering to teach the disciples what true giving was about. The impoverished woman had given more than anyone else at the temple that day, because she had given all that she had.

Mark's Closing Remarks

Mark closed his Gospel with the resurrection of Christ, the empty tomb, and the angel explaining to the women (and to the world through Mark) that Jesus was, indeed, dead but had come back to life and was still all about doing God's business. This is the very thing Mark had set out to reveal all along.

SCRIPTURE BITS

A Revolutionary View

So Jesus called [the disciples] together and said, "You know that in this world kings are tyrants, and officials lord it over the people beneath them. But among you it should be quite different. Whoever wants to be a leader among you must be your servant, and whoever wants to be first must be the slave of all. For even I, the Son of Man, came here not to be served but to serve others, and to give my life as a ransom for many."

Mark 10:42–45 NLT

LUKE

IN CONTEXT

Here's the scoop. . .

Written: *around* A.D. 60

Written by: *Luke*

Writing style: *a biographical narrative*

One-liner: *Amazing news! Jesus is God and yet totally human. He understands our journey.*

The Good Doctor

Matthew, the disciple and former tax collector, wrote to convince the Jewish people that Jesus was the promised Messiah. Mark, the missionary sidekick, wrote to convince the Romans that Jesus was a servant and a Savior. Luke, the doctor, writes to convince his Greek friend, Theophilus, that Jesus was God, but also fully and completely human. In other words, since we couldn't reconcile with God on our own, He became one of us to accomplish the task.

> *Having carefully investigated all of these accounts from the beginning, I have decided to write a careful summary for you, to reassure you of the truth of all you were taught. (Luke 1:3–4 NLT)*

There's a lot of joy in the opening of Luke. Zechariah, an old priest, is happy that his wife will finally bear a child. Mary the mother of Jesus is happy that God has chosen to use her. Elizabeth, Zechariah's wife, is happy that she and Mary are pregnant with boys that will make a difference for God. Zechariah is even happier when he finally gets his voice back after the birth of his son John.

The angels were happy when they told the shepherds that Jesus was finally born. The shepherds were happy enough to travel into the city and greet this baby-king.

When Mary and Joseph took Jesus to the temple to dedicate their baby, they met two older people, Anna and Simeon, who recognized that Jesus wasn't just any baby, and they celebrated right then and there. There was a sacred party going on.

Luke's Strategy

Because Luke was writing from the perspective of the wonder of Jesus' humanity, he included some interesting facts that the other Gospel writers didn't include. He gave insights into Christ's childhood. He documented Christ's compassion in dealing with the people around Him. Luke's Gospel made the point that Jesus wasn't too high and mighty to get down and dirty when ministry demanded it. His priority was becoming a part of our journey and teaching us a better way.

Luke revealed to us Jesus' friendships. He mentioned more women than any other Gospel. He revealed to us that Jesus really was God come to earth to walk many hard miles in our sandals. Luke revealed to us a Jesus that ultimately died so that we could find forgiveness.

The Luke Exclusive

Here are some stories that Luke included that none of the other Gospel writers included. These stories offered insight into Jesus' everyday life.

Jesus visited two friends, Mary and Martha, in their home. Martha was an organizer and was running around breathless. Mary was an admirer and spent her time sitting at Jesus' feet. When Martha complained, Jesus affirmed Mary's choice, to just be with Him (Luke 10:38–42).

One day Jesus was teaching His disciples within earshot of the Pharisees, religious leaders who had (more often than not) made a business of their piety. These leaders loved money, and more than that they loved looking righteous. In their presence Jesus told a story about some workers who were given the responsibility to invest their boss's money while he was out of town. Some of the workers invested in the wrong kinds of things, or just

IN CONTEXT

Matthew opened with a genealogy because that's what would matter to his audience. Mark opened with Jesus' adult ministry because that's what would matter to his audience. Luke opened with a whole lot of celebration. Maybe that's what Theophilus needed to hear. Maybe it's what we need to hear as well.

SCRIPTURE BITS

If I've heard it once. . .

These verses have appeared everywhere from rural church Christmas pageants to Charlie Brown's Christmas special. All from Luke's commitment to his friend, Theophilus, knowing who Jesus was.

Now there were in the same country shepherds living out in the fields, keeping watch over their flock by night. And behold, an angel of the Lord stood before them, and the glory of the Lord shone around them, and they were greatly afraid. Then the angel said to them, "Do not be afraid, for behold, I bring you good tidings of great joy which will be to all people. For there is born to you this day in the city of David a Savior, who is Christ the Lord. And this will be the sign to you: You will find a Babe wrapped in swaddling cloths, lying in a manger." And suddenly there was with the angel a multitude of the heavenly host praising God and saying: "Glory to God in the highest, And on earth peace, goodwill toward men!" So it was, when the angels had gone away from them into heaven, that the shepherds said to one another, "Let us now go to Bethlehem and see this thing that has come to pass, which the Lord has made known to us." And they came with haste and found Mary and Joseph, and the Babe lying in a manger. Now when they had seen Him, they made widely known the saying which was told them concerning this Child. And all those who heard it marveled at those things which were told them by the shepherds. But Mary kept all these things and pondered them in her heart. Then the shepherds returned, glorifying and praising God for all the things that they had heard and seen, as it was told them.

Luke 2:8–20 NKJV

didn't invest at all. Then when their boss came back, he held them account-able. They didn't have much to say for their lives (Luke 16:1–17:10). Jesus didn't win any points with the Pharisees that day.

Then there was the day that ten, count 'em, ten lepers came to Jesus to be healed. Jesus healed them and sent them to the priest to be proclaimed well. Out of the ten, only one came back to express his gratitude. Jesus asked him, with perhaps a twinkle in His eye, something like: "Now weren't there ten of you? Where are your buddies?" (Luke 17:11–19)

Jesus told two parables about prayer that only Luke recorded. In the first, a widow came to a judge to ask for a judgment against her enemy. She was a woman and she was a widow, so she was not high on the power scale or the social ladder. Because of her perseverance, though, the judge finally granted her request. Jesus' message? Don't stop praying.

In the second parable, two men went to pray at the temple. One was proud and prayed to be seen by others. The other was humble and prayed to be forgiven by God. What was the point? The humble man was the one God heard (Luke 18:1–14).

JOHN

IN CONTEXT

Here's the scoop. . .

Written: *around* A.D. *90*

Written by: *John, the disciple*

Writing style: *a biographical profile*

One-liner: *It really is true. Jesus Christ is God Himself.*

John's Gospel

John wrote his Gospel after Matthew, Mark, and Luke's were already written. The first three Gospels had a lot of similarities. The Book of John added some variety.

Matthew opened with a genealogy. Mark opened with the beginning of Jesus' adult ministry. Luke opened with the celebration of Jesus' birth. John opened with a symbolic, almost poetic, definitely philosophic introduction of Jesus at the very creation of the world.

> *In the beginning was the Word, and the Word was with God, and the Word was God. He was with God in the beginning. Through him all things were made; without him nothing was made that has been made. In him was life, and that life was the light of men.*
>
> *The Word became flesh and made his dwelling among us. We have seen his glory, the glory of the One and Only, who came from the Father, full of grace and truth. (John 1:1–4, 14 NIV)*

John established Jesus' deity by revealing that He created the very world in which we live.

The Incarnation

When Jesus became man and took on a human body, it is called the "incarnation" (you've probably heard reincarnation more than just incarnation). It was and still is a mystery. How can someone be fully God and fully person? It takes faith to believe.

If God wasn't fully human, His death for our sins wouldn't mean the same thing. He wouldn't have been one of us. If He wasn't fully God, His death for our sins wouldn't mean anything, either. One person can't just decide to take a punishment for the whole world. It takes God, the creator of the universe, to decide that.

Only in John

Here are some stories from the life of Jesus that you can find only in the Gospel of John.

John is the only Gospel that recorded Jesus' first miracle at a wedding in Cana. They ran out of wine. At the request of His mother, and with a little negotiation between them, Jesus changed some plain old well water into wine so the host wouldn't be embarrassed (John 2:1–11).

From the beginning of His ministry, Jesus ferociously confronted the men who made the temple into a marketplace. He defended the temple as his own territory (John 2:12–25).

An enlightened Pharisee, Nicodemus, came to Jesus at night to find out if He was for real. It was during this conversation that Jesus firmly established the concept of being "born again." It's also where Jesus spoke the famous words we now know as John 3:16—God so loved the world, that He gave His only Son… (John 3:1–21).

IN CONTEXT

Matthew focused on Christ's Messiah-ship, which was a very Jewish issue. Mark focused on Jesus as a servant. Luke focused on Christ's humanity, even though He was deity. John focused on Jesus as the Son of God, His deity even though He was human.

You may have heard the story that is often called the story of the woman at the well. Besides being a woman (in a culture that devalued women), this woman was a Samaritan (with whom the Jewish people had a major racial conflict). Her conversation with Jesus revealed His lack of concern for status and His love for humans in general (John 4:1–42).

In an amazing account, Jesus was confronted by the religious leaders with a woman who was caught in adultery (which at that time was punishable by death). Because of the absence of the man who had been caught as well, and because of the political climate, Jesus recognized this confrontation as a trap. Rather than condemn her, Jesus confronted the sin in the lives of the accusers (John 8:1–11).

Jesus raised Lazarus, His friend, from the dead, just by calling out his name (John 11:1–44).

SCRIPTURE BITS

John's Bottom Line

But although the world was made through him, the world didn't recognize him when he came. Even in his own land and among his own people, he was not accepted. But to all who believed him and accepted him, he gave the right to become children of God. They are reborn! This is not a physical birth resulting from human passion or plan— this rebirth comes from God. So the Word [Jesus] became human and lived here on earth among us. He was full of unfailing love and faithfulness. And we have seen his glory, the glory of the only Son of the Father.

John 1:10–14 NLT

HISTORY BOOK

After the life and ministry of Jesus Christ, the New Testament focuses on the church, the followers that Jesus left behind to do His work. We often think of this period of history as archaic. After all, they didn't even have big buses to carry youth groups on mission trips! But if you'll look closely, they were pretty organized for a world that had just figured out that they needed to use antiseptic on wounds.

ACTS

IN CONTEXT

Here's the scoop...

Written: *around* A.D. *65*

Written by: *Luke (the same Luke that wrote the Gospel)*

Writing style: *a chronological narrative*

One-liner: *A new church organizes: Jesus' sacrifice makes us right with God. Spread the news!*

Walking Across Acts

The Book of Acts is a sequel to the Book of Luke and is a bridge between the Gospels and the epistles (or letters) of the New Testament. The Gospels contain the story of Jesus' life and ministry. The epistles contain encouragement and training for the early church. The Book of Acts records how the church got organized from a group of bewildered disciples into the "body of Christ" in the world.

Pentecost

Just after Jesus returned to heaven (this was after His death and resurrection), the Jewish people were scheduled to celebrate an annual feast called Pentecost. As they gathered together, an unexpected and wonderful thing happened. The Holy Spirit came. This was a huge event.

Jesus had given the disciples a promise about this: " *'The Counselor, the Holy Spirit, whom the Father will send in my name, will teach you all things and will remind you of everything I have said to you.' "* (John 14:26)

If you close your eyes and imagine what it would cost a special effects team to recreate this event, it puts it into a little better perspective.

> *On the day of Pentecost, seven weeks after Jesus' resurrection, the believers were meeting together in one place. Suddenly, there was a sound from heaven like the roaring of a mighty windstorm in the skies above them, and*

> it filled the house where they were meeting. Then, what looked like flames
> or tongues of fire appeared and settled on each of them. And everyone pre-
> sent was filled with the Holy Spirit and began speaking in other languages,
> as the Holy Spirit gave them this ability.
>
> Godly Jews from many nations were living in Jerusalem at that time.
> When they heard this sound, they came running to see what it was all
> about, and they were bewildered to hear their own languages being spoken
> by the believers.
>
> They were beside themselves with wonder. "How can this be?" they
> exclaimed. "These people are all from Galilee, and yet we hear them speak-
> ing the languages of the lands where we were born!" (Acts 2:1–8 NLT)

Do you understand the significance of this event? In the Old Testament, people, even believers, related to God mostly in the temple. It wasn't that God
was any different. He was everywhere and wherever He wanted to be. But
He was revealed to humanity through a holy place or a pillar of fire or a burning bush. Then God came to humanity as Jesus, to accomplish His own sacrifice. But at Pentecost God came to humanity to make His home in each of us.
It was a whole different way of experiencing God's presence and power.

This was the beginning of the early church. At this point those who
believed in Jesus' resurrection began to get organized. They began to determine specific ministry roles. They began to share their money and posses-
sions with those who didn't have any. They began to organize to go out and
share the news of Jesus' forgiveness through His death. Everything was fresh
and new. The rules had all changed. The church was changing with them.

The Early Church

The early believers did the only thing they knew to do: They loved each
other and shared the news of Christ's sacrifice and God's forgiveness. And
they got organized to accomplish the mission that Jesus left with them—to
tell the world.

One of the main leaders of the early church was, surprisingly, the disciple
Peter. He was the guy who, during Jesus' trial, denied he even knew Christ.
Yet, after Pentecost, Peter became a mainstay of early church leadership.

It's interesting to note that the same religious leaders who had opposed
Jesus when He was on earth, opposed the early church. They persecuted
the apostles. From the perspective of these leaders, they were trying to

A Mind-Blower

During the crucifixion of Christ, the Bible records a specific event that happened in the temple. It's almost easy to miss in Luke's Gospel nestled between all the intense events surrounding Jesus' death. Here it is:

> By this time it was noon, and darkness fell across the whole land until three o'clock. The light from the sun was gone. And suddenly, the thick veil hanging in the Temple was torn apart. Then Jesus shouted, "Father, I entrust my spirit into your hands!" And with those words he breathed his last.
>
> (Luke 23:44–46 NLT)

The veil that tore in the temple was the curtain that separated the Holy of Holies (which was the place where God was supposed to dwell) from the place where the people came to sacrifice and worship. Do you get what that means? It's really the main event leading into the coming of the Holy Spirit in Acts.

One of the names Jesus was given was Emmanuel. That meant "God with us." When Jesus came, God was with humanity in a whole new and different way. He walked among us. He dealt with our same circumstances and feelings. But at Jesus' death, God came even closer. Do you get that? When the curtain tore and then the Holy Spirit came, it meant that God was in us and with us like never before.

It wasn't that God changed, but it was a whole new way of our understanding His presence and experiencing His life and knowing Him.

It was an atomic bomb of revelation. God with us. God in us. A whole new life of faith.

Wow. It gets me every time.

stamp out heresy. They didn't believe that Jesus was the Messiah. They also didn't want to lose the power and prestige they enjoyed in their community.

Mission Trips

Once the church had their main base organized, it was time to spread out. Acts recorded several "missionary journeys" in which Paul and others spread the good news that Christ had risen from the dead and could forgive sin once and for all.

Missionary Journey #1

Paul and Barnabas made this journey together. Barnabas was one of the Christians who was brave enough to befriend Paul soon after his conversion. (Before his conversion, he persecuted and killed Christians.) Paul and Barnabas traveled together from Antioch to Cyprus and then Galatia. The New Testament book, Galatians, was written by Paul back to the churches he had helped on this journey.

Missionary Journey #2

Paul took a team of missionaries with him on this second journey: Silas, Luke, and Timothy. They visited Philippi, Thessalonica, Berea, Corinth, and Athens. You may recognize several books of the Bible that were written back to these churches: Philippians, 1 and 2 Thessalonians, and 1 and 2 Corinthians.

Missionary Journey #3

Paul went to Ephesus for a lengthy stay (he later wrote a letter to the churches there: Ephesians), then traveled back through Greece and to Jerusalem.

Remember the Context

By the time the three missionary journeys were completed, Christianity was raising quite a ruckus. The message and life of Jesus Christ had upset everyone from the Jewish religious leaders to the Roman emperors (who saw themselves as gods to be worshipped).

After the third missionary journey, Paul was put in jail. What the government had in mind was to squelch Paul's influence. So what did the

IN CONTEXT

The Jew v. Gentile Revolution

If you remember anything about the Old Testament, you should remember that most of it is about the history of the Jewish nation. Their whole story came out of a promise God made to a man named Abraham. Their prophets constantly promised them a Messiah, a deliverer.

With such a rich history, it isn't surprising that the Jewish people who accepted Christ's deity didn't really want to share Him with the non-Jewish world. He was their promised Messiah, after all. If anyone wanted to accept Christ's substitution for his sin, let him be circumcised and become a Jew!

During Acts, God was consistently breaking down these barriers. No one needed to become a Jew. Jesus had completed what the Jewish law required. Now it was time for everyone to have access to God just because of his or her faith in Christ. God's original promise to Abraham (father of the Jewish nation) was completed through Jesus' life and work. Faith in what Christ did, rather than nationality or ritual, was now the issue in being accepted by God. This was a HUGE concept for the people of that day to take in.

We take for granted this kind of thinking today: God's love for everyone. But at that time, it was a major shift in thought and probably a scary one for these people who had suffered so much to believe.

It truly was a revolution.

government do? They transported him to Rome, the center of all commerce and communication! They placed him under house arrest (which allowed him visitors), and he basically set up a base of operations right under their noses. He wrote many of the letters we know as the epistles of the New Testament and encouraged Christians everywhere.

Eventually Paul was killed for his faith, but until then he didn't miss an opportunity to share the news that had really turned the world on its ear: Jesus Christ was the Son of God and gave Himself for our sins.

THE LETTERS (OR EPISTLES)

Talk about invasion of privacy. This section of the Bible is made up of somebody else's mail! As the early church was organizing, they had no access to e-mail or telephone, so the snail-est of mail (often carried by foot) was the best communication process they had. You can imagine the excitement when a town received a letter back from Paul after he had started a church there. They probably read it, reread it, passed it around, and almost wore it out (no copiers, either, remember).

The writers of these letters had a similar role with the early church that the prophets had with the Old Testament Hebrews. The prophets spoke out and said, "Since God is God and the Messiah is coming, we should live this way." The New Testament church leaders said, "Since God is God and Jesus came to provide a sacrifice, we should live this way." One was faith through foresight and the other was faith through hindsight.

We know the first thirteen of these letters are from Paul. The first nine are to churches. The next four are to people. The second letter to Timothy is probably the last letter Paul wrote before his death. This is some pretty significant mail to get to sift through.

THE EPISTLES

- Romans
- 1 & 2 Corinthians
- Galatians
- Ephesians
- Philippians
- Colossians
- 1 & 2 Thessalonians
- 1 & 2 Timothy
- Titus
- Philemon
- Hebrews
- James
- 1 & 2 Peter
- 1, 2, & 3 John
- Jude

ROMANS

Here's the scoop. . .

Written: *around* A.D. *60*

Written by: *Paul, the apostle*

Writing style: *a letter of explanation*

One-liner: *Dear Roman church: The only way we can be right with God is through faith. Paul*

What It All Means

Paul wrote to the Romans in preparation for his trip there. He wanted them to know as much as possible up front. That way, when he arrived they could spend their time together digging deeper into their understanding of what Jesus Christ's life and death meant.

While the Book of Romans isn't a stuffy book, it is a doctrinal book. It is a book that lays out the logic of Christianity:

- We all have a fatal human flaw—we sin, we choose ourselves over God—we are spiritually dead (Romans 3:23).

- No matter how many good things we try to do to cover up this flaw, they do not make us clean before God. He wants us to be in relationship with Him. The good things we do, do not make us spiritually alive (Romans 5:12).

- Jesus came as a sacrifice for all of our sin; He took our punishment. He died a physical death so we could have a spiritual rebirth (Romans 5:21).

- Because He did that, we can have an open and loving relationship with God—we can be spiritually alive—even though we are still flawed humans who struggle with our self-centeredness (Romans 6:5–7).

- Before we can be really alive spiritually, we have to believe that only

through Christ's death and resurrection can we have this new life. It is
an act of faith in this gift God offers (Romans 5:1–2).

- God gives us this new life only through this act of faith. We can't earn
  it. We can't buy it. We can't deserve it. We can't bring ourselves to life
  spiritually. Only God can do that for us—if we believe (Romans 11:6).

Pretty cool stuff.

The Reformation

You might remember a period of history called the Reformation. This religious movement was begun by Martin Luther. (Not Martin Luther King Jr.
That was a different period of history.) Martin Luther didn't mean to start
the Reformation. He didn't wake up one day and say, "Well, today is a good
day for a revolution." Actually all he did was read the Book of Romans.

During Martin Luther's day, people worked harder and harder to try and
make themselves right before God. Many of the church leadership exploited
this desire to "work your way to heaven." People were even buying what
they thought was forgiveness—with mere money! When Martin Luther read
the Book of Romans, he realized, "It's not about being good enough or
working hard enough. It's about God's grace. He gave us a gift in Christ's
death, and He just asks that we believe that He did it."

Martin Luther started preaching that message and it started a revolution
of thought that we now call the Reformation. It changed the way the world
did church, and things have never been the same.

SCRIPTURE BITS

A Famous Verse in Romans

And we know that God causes everything to work together for the good of those who love God and are called according to his purpose for them. For God knew his people in advance, and he chose them to become like his Son, so that his Son would be the firstborn, with many brothers and sisters. And having chosen them, he called them to come to him. And he gave them right standing with himself, and he promised them his glory.

Romans 8:28–30 NLT

1 CORINTHIANS

IN CONTEXT

Here's the scoop. . .

Written: *around* A.D. 55

Written by: *Paul, the apostle*

Writing style: *a letter of instruction*

One-liner: *Dear church, Don't be like the world around you. Be who God made you to be, pure and effective.*

The Corinthian Church

Paul had helped start the church at Corinth. The Corinthian church had a lot of challenges because Corinth was one wicked city. In that day there was a phrase, "to live like a Corinthian," which meant to be immoral. In fact, if there was a character in a play who was known to be a Corinthian, he almost always walked on stage drunk.

Also, Corinth was a really important trade center. It was located on a thin strip of land between two oceans. One of the unique things about Corinth was a track that led from one of these oceans to the other. If certain ships didn't want to have to sail around the land, they could load their ships onto this track and carry their boats and cargo to the other side. (Who said it was not a technological age, huh?)

Because of its immorality and because of its great location for spreading the gospel, Corinth really needed a church. The problem, though, was that it was difficult for the church there to not get sucked back into the evil and (dare I say it?) debauchery around them.

Evidently, when Paul wrote this letter, the church wasn't doing too well at the not-getting-sucked-back-in thing. Husbands and wives were not being faithful. People in the church were not getting along. Things were getting pretty messy. Because of this, the church wrote Paul. What we call the "Book" of 1 Corinthians is actually Paul's letter in response.

The Issues at Hand

There are several passages in 1 Corinthians that have been so relevant to the church in every generation that if you hear enough sermons, you are going to hear something from these passages. They show us that the issues we face in church today are not much different than the issues the early church faced. Cultures change, but human nature is human nature.

1. Division and Disagreements

What I mean is this: One of you says, "I follow Paul"; another, "I follow Apollos"; another, "I follow Cephas"; still another, "I follow Christ." Is Christ divided? Was Paul crucified for you? Were you baptized into the name of Paul? (1 Corinthians 1:12–13)

Instead of following Jesus, the Corinthians were doing what people still do today. They were stargazing. They were focusing on Christian celebrities. They were forming spiritual cliques. They were following men, usually the man who introduced them to the faith. Paul directed their faith back to the only place it belonged—Jesus Christ, God-in-the-flesh.

2. Right and Wrong

The Corinthian church was surrounded by a culture much like our own in which sexual purity (abstinence outside of marriage) was not "in."

Your own members are aware that there is sexual sin going on among them. This kind of sin is not even heard of among unbelievers—a man is actually married to his father's wife. (1 Corinthians 5:1 GOD'S WORD)

Stay away from sexual sins. Other sins that people commit don't affect their bodies the same way sexual sins do. People who sin sexually sin against their own bodies. (1 Corinthians 6:18 GOD'S WORD)

It's easy for a church to be influenced by the culture around it. The Corinthian church lived in a land flowing over with "everybody's doing it." Paul reminded them to follow the teachings of Christ, even if it meant giving up destructive behaviors that they enjoyed. (Anything relevant to contemporary culture there?)

3. Spiritual Gifts

In chapter 12 of 1 Corinthians, Paul explained the concept of spiritual gifts. He said that each person had a gift given through the Holy Spirit. The purpose of the gift was "for the common good." In other words we all have something to offer, some ability that God can use to make the world a better place.

Paul had to remind the Corinthians that their gifts didn't do anyone any good if they were bickering and fighting over them. His words are telling us the same thing today.

SCRIPTURE BITS

What the World Needs Now Is Love. . .

1 Corinthians 13 gives us a description of true love.

Love is patient,
  love is kind.
It does not envy,
  it does not boast,
  it is not proud.
It is not rude,
  it is not self-seeking,
  it is not easily angered,
  it keeps no record of wrongs.
Love does not delight in evil
  but rejoices with the truth.
It always protects,
  always trusts,
  always hopes,
  always perseveres.
Love never fails.

1 Corinthians 13:4–8

2 CORINTHIANS

Here's the scoop. . .

Written: *around* A.D. 55

Written by: *Paul, the apostle*

Writing style: *a personal letter*

One-liner: *Dear church, Here's who I am. Now let me tell you who you should be.*

The Situation

Have you ever tried to work out a conflict long-distance? It's difficult, isn't it? All the he-saids, she-saids seem impossible to control through phone calls or e-mail or letters.

That's the kind of battle Paul was fighting when he wrote 2 Corinthians. He had helped start the church at Corinth on one of his missionary journeys. After leaving, though, he heard about some shaky situations there. That caused him to write 1 Corinthians. It was a firm and confrontational letter.

After that, things seemed to calm down. Then Paul started hearing that people in the church were criticizing him and actually trying to discredit him. He wrote them again. This time his letter was very personal and less confrontational. This time he let them know more of who he was than just what he thought. He opened his heart a bit and let them know of his love and his commitment to them.

Standing Up for Himself

Because there were people discrediting him, Paul stood up for himself to the Corinthians. He traced his path in ministry. He established the experiences that had allowed him to be used by God. He walked that thin line between bragging and just telling it like it is.

Paul knew that in order to continue ministering to the church at Corinth, he needed to stand up to his detractors. That's exactly what he did in 2 Corinthians.

A Good Lesson

There's a good lesson for us in what happened between Paul's first and second letters to the Corinthians. Paul's first letter was a strong confrontational letter. The Corinthians could have become resentful. They could have gotten even worse than they were. They could have gotten defensive. But when you look at Paul's second letter, you see that he was praising them. They heard the truth and they changed according to it. That's to their credit…and a good lesson for us.

GALATIANS

IN CONTEXT

Here's the scoop. . .

Written: *around* A.D. *50*

Written by: *Paul, the apostle*

Writing style: *a letter of instruction and explanation*

One-liner: *Dear church, You can't earn God's approval by obeying rules. It takes faith.*

Freedom vs. Chains

When Paul visited Galatia, he explained Christianity to people who were not Jewish people. After he left, though, these new Christians were influenced by people called "Judaizers." The Judaizers believed that anyone who wanted to be a Christian should become a Jew, or at least observe Jewish customs and law, like circumcision and keeping kosher and yearly feasts.

The problem was not the Jewish customs so much as the attitude that a person couldn't be a Christian unless he or she observed these customs. If that were true, then salvation was about more than grace and faith—it was about earning your righteousness. Paul wrote,

> *I am astonished that you are so quickly deserting the one who called you by the grace of Christ and are turning to a different gospel—which is really no gospel at all. (Galatians 1:6–7)*

It was because of the influence of the Judaizers that Paul wrote the Book of Galatians. He wrote to emphasize that the grace of God is free, absolutely free. There is nothing anyone can do to deserve it or earn it. If we think we can, then we lock ourselves up in chains of obedience to something that really doesn't matter.

Galatians, the Cousin to Romans

In many ways Galatians has the same message as Romans. Galatians is shorter, though, and not so technical. In both letters Paul tries to make the point that God's grace, His love-no-matter-what-we've-done, is free for those who believe in Him. It doesn't do any good to try and earn it. "Earning it" is not what Christianity is about. Christianity is about "believing it."

SCRIPTURE BITS

To Pay or Not to Pay

Sometimes it's easier to feel like we can earn God's love and acceptance. After all, if He gives it to us for free, we don't feel like we've paid our dues. No matter what feels good to us, though, we can never be good enough or perfect enough to really deserve God's approval. Getting it for free, out of His grace, is the only way we're ever going to get it.

Christ is useless to you if you are counting on clearing your debt to God by keeping those laws; you are lost from God's grace.

Galatians 5:4 TLB

EPHESIANS

Here's the scoop. . .

Written: *around* A.D. *60*

Written by: *Paul, the apostle (from prison!)*

Writing style: *a letter of encouragement*

One-liner: *Dear church, Receive God's amazing love for you. Then, love each other well.*

Just Checking In

We know Paul was in prison in Rome when he wrote this letter. We know that he had Tychicus (who delivered Colossians and Philemon) deliver it. We just don't know exactly why Paul wrote to this church at this time. For all we know he was just checking in, tending a garden that he had helped plant. It was a good thing for us that he did.

Ephesians is a beautiful letter full of profound and meaningful thoughts. If you are one of those people who keep a pen with their Bible to underline the verses that really jump out at you, you'll underline a lot of Ephesians.

An Encouraging Word

The first part of the Book of Ephesians is a lesson in encouragement. It is a wonderful reminder of God's love and grace. Some verses remind us of the truths of some of Paul's other letters:

> *Because of his kindness you have been saved through trusting Christ. And even trusting is not of yourselves; it too is a gift from God.*
> *(Ephesians 2:8 TLB)*

It's difficult to read Ephesians without feeling loved and so fortunate to be a part of God's family.

Long ago, even before he made the world, God chose us to be his very own, through what Christ would do for us; he decided then to make us holy in his eyes, without a single fault—we who stand before him covered with his love. His unchanging plan has always been to adopt us into his own family by sending Jesus Christ to die for us. And he did this because he wanted to! (Ephesians 1:4–5 TLB)

It's a big enough deal to realize that God offers us an opportunity to know Him and to be loved by Him. It's even bigger to realize that God really has had our adoption into His family planned from the beginning of the world. His intentions toward us have never changed, starting before Genesis and continuing on through today.

Basically, by telling the church all this, Paul was just loving up on them, letting them know that God didn't love them sparingly. Instead God lavished love on them. Who doesn't need to read that?

> **GOOD NEWS**
> When someone becomes a Christian he becomes a brand new person inside. He is not the same any more. A new life has begun!
>
> **2 Corinthians 5:17** TLB

The Church

The last part of Ephesians focused more specifically on how the people of the church loved each other. He wrote about the gifts that each person brings. He wrote about basic decency: being truthful with each other, not stealing. He wrote about who the church should be in the world—Christ's body, the physical manifestation of God. When you think about it, that's a mind-blower. Just as surely as God put on a human form as Christ so that we could see Him, now the church is that body so that the world can still see God.

If the church lived together the way that Paul describes in the Book of Ephesians, what a great reflection of God we would be.

SCRIPTURE BITS

What the Church Is All About

Be humble and gentle. Be patient with each other, making allowance for each other's faults because of your love. Try always to be led along together by the Holy Spirit, and so be at peace with one another.

We are all parts of one body, we have the same Spirit, and we have all been called to the same glorious future. For us there is only one Lord, one faith, one baptism, and we all have the same God and Father who is over us all and in us all, and living through every part of us. However, Christ has given each of us special abilities—whatever he wants us to have out of his rich storehouse of gifts.

Ephesians 4:2–7 TLB

Stop being mean, bad-tempered and angry. Quarreling, harsh words, and dislike of others should have no place in your lives. Instead, be kind to each other, tenderhearted, forgiving one another, just as God has forgiven you because you belong to Christ.

Follow God's example in everything you do just as a much loved child imitates his father.

Ephesians 4:31–5:1 TLB

PHILIPPIANS

IN CONTEXT

Here's the scoop. . .

Written: *around* A.D. *60*

Written by: *Paul, the apostle (from prison!)*

Writing style: *a thank-you note*

One-liner: *Dear church, Knowing you brings me joy. Knowing God brings us all joy.*

Old Friends Are the Best

Paul (with Silas, Timothy, and Luke) founded the church at Philippi on his second missionary journey. It was the first European church founded by Paul and it was the push of the gospel into a predominantly Gentile culture. Philippi was located on a plain. It was a central location for all the roads in northern Greece. Because of this, it was a strategic location for the gospel to take hold.

The church at Philippi was an old friend for Paul. They supported Paul in his ministry. In fact Philippians is partly a thank-you note from Paul for their financial support.

Be Joyful

Philippians was a letter of joy. It was the kind of letter that had you smiling all the way back from the mailbox. Even though Paul wrote Philippians to thank them for their kindness, he took the opportunity to give a little lesson with his thank you.

Paul's lesson came first from his own life. He was chained to a Roman guard while he was writing, for goodness' sake! He was in jail, yet he was writing about joy. Here are some of his key points for the Philippians.

- Have integrity (Philippians 1:27).

- Be humble (Philippians 2:3–4).

- Be positive (Philippians 2:14).

- Remember what matters (Philippians 3:13–14).

- Be content (Philippians 4:11–12).

Paul's letter to the Philippians reads almost like a letter written to the folks back home. Paul tells them thanks and then tells them stuff that's important to him, just because it is.

SCRIPTURE BITS

Philippians is a book full of verses that make you go "Hmmmmmm." Here's one:

I have learned to be content whatever the circumstances. I know what it is to be in need, and I know what it is to have plenty. I have learned the secret of being content in any and every situation, whether well fed or hungry, whether living in plenty or in want.

Philippians 4:11–12

I no longer count on my own goodness or my ability to obey God's law, but I trust Christ to save me. For God's way of making us right with himself depends on faith.

Philippians 3:9 NLT

COLOSSIANS

Here's the scoop. . .

Written: *around* A.D. *60*

Written by: *Paul, the apostle*

Writing style: *a letter of correction*

One-liner: *Dear church, Faith in Christ is enough. Don't add anything else to it.*

Influenced by Modern Culture

The city of Colossae was a cultural and philosophical mixture, a melting pot. The Colossians claimed a variety of religions and variations within each. Paul had evidently heard that the church at Colossae was being influenced by the culture around them. Paul called these influences heresies. They included:

- Worshiping angels

- Believing rules and regulations could create righteousness

- Trusting personal goodness instead of God's goodness

- Trusting philosophical prowess and intellectual arrogance

Paul wrote this letter to simplify and clarify exactly what faith does and is. His message was simple: All of this "stuff" you're adding on has nothing to do with your faith. Knowing who Jesus was—that was the most important thing.

The Colossians were being tempted by the same thing that tempts the church today: They were trying to make their relationship with God more complicated. Life is hard enough without making it even more complicated! But somehow we humans find a way to do it. Maybe we feel like we need more of a system than "God has made a way for you—believe, love, and obey him." Throughout history we have struggled with letting faith in God be enough. The church at Colossae was adding parts of their culture into their faith because it was fashionable. They were not the first church to struggle with this mix-and-match kind of faith and they were definitely not the last.

SCRIPTURE BITS

The Gospel According to Colossians

Don't let others spoil your faith and joy with their philosophies, their wrong and shallow answers built on men's thoughts and ideas, instead of on what Christ has said. For in Christ there is all of God in a human body, so you have everything when you have Christ, and you are filled with God through your union with Christ. He is the highest Ruler, with authority over every other power.

Colossians 2:8–10 TLB

1 THESSALONIANS

Here's the scoop...

Written: *around* A.D. *50*

Written by: *Paul, the apostle*

Writing style: *a letter of instruction and encouragement*

One-liner: *Dear church, Look forward to Christ's return!*

Hard Times

Being a Christian at the time this letter was written was not a lot of fun. Today Christians wear cool T-shirts with spiritual sayings, and they attend large conferences where they learn more and more about the life they should live. Not so in Paul's day. Being a Christian was unpopular and even outlawed in some places. When someone became a Christian, he often had to leave his family behind and live in hiding. Christians needed all the encouragement they could get to keep the faith.

That's much of the reason Paul wrote to the Christians at Thessalonica. He couldn't make their situation any easier, and he couldn't promise them it wouldn't get worse before it got better. So he promised them the only thing he could. He promised them that one day Jesus would return and He would make things okay. In fact, this book has one of the most famous Bible passages about Jesus' return to the earth:

> *For the Lord himself will come down from heaven with a mighty shout and with the soul-stirring cry of the archangel and the great trumpet-call of God. And the believers who are dead will be the first to rise to meet the Lord. Then we who are still alive and remain on the earth will be caught up with them in the clouds to meet the Lord in the air and remain with him forever. So comfort and encourage each other with this news.*
>
> *When is all this going to happen? I really don't need to say anything about that, dear brothers, for you know perfectly well that no one knows. That day of the Lord will come unexpectedly like a thief in the night.*
> (1 Thessalonians 4:16–5:2 TLB)

Second Coming?

When Jesus left the earth after His resurrection He promised to come again. The people who heard Him make those promises believed that would happen during their lifetime. The Thessalonians lived in that generation. Almost every generation since then has thought the same thing. Because we are still waiting for that return, which many call the second coming, Paul's word of encouragement to them applies to us as well.

2 THESSALONIANS

IN CONTEXT

Here's the scoop. . .

Written: *around* A.D. 50

Written by: *Paul, the apostle*

Writing style: *a letter of clarification*

One-liner: *Dear church, Look forward to Christ's return, but keep living full lives and working hard!*

Oops! Church Overboard!

Now, it is true that when Christ returns it is going to be an amazing event, but when the bills come due, we need to be responsible to pay them. These Thessalonians were so consumed with that one event that they were letting go of their lives on earth. Paul needed to set them straight.

That was the first problem, but there was another related problem. Since the hanger-outers didn't have anything to do and were bored, they began to do what people do when they are hanging out and bored. They began to make trouble, gossip, become busybodies, and get into everyone else's business. They began to mooch off each other because they had no money to pay their own bills.

That is why Paul wrote his second letter to the Thessalonian church. He needed to pull them back to center, back to a balance.

Yet we hear that some of you are living idle lives, refusing to work and wasting time meddling in other people's business. In the name of the Lord Jesus Christ, we appeal to such people—no, we command them: Settle down and get to work. Earn your own living. (2 Thessalonians 3:11–12 NLT)

1 TIMOTHY

Here's the scoop...

Written: *around* A.D. 65

Written by: *Paul, the apostle*

Writing style: *a personal letter*

One-liner: *Dear Tim, You're doing well. Here are some things to remember about leading a church.*

Like a Son

Timothy was an up-and-comer in the early church. We don't know much about his dad except that he was Greek. Timothy's mom was Jewish. One of the most well-known things about Timothy is that his mom (Lois) and his grandmom (Eunice) were big influences on his faith. Paul even mentions them in his second letter to Timothy.

At the time when Paul wrote this letter, Timothy was in Ephesus helping lead the church. Timothy and Paul had traveled to Ephesus together. Paul left Timothy there to keep the church on track. Remember that, at that point, churches didn't have big buildings and programs. The church was simply groups of people meeting at different places, often homes, around town. Timothy's greatest challenge in Ephesus was the mixture of philosophy and thoughts that continually pulled people away from the simple truth of the gospel. Because of that, Paul wrote much about how to stay away from heresy.

Paul wrote this letter to encourage Timothy and to train him a little. It is a straightforward letter that is chock-full of advice for a young Christian (or any age Christian, really) who wants to serve God in a meaningful way.

In this letter Paul covers some of the same ground that he touches on in other letters, such as:

- Worship

- False teachers

- Church leadership

Paul had invested so much in their relationship that Timothy was like a son to him. That's why in this first letter to Timothy, Paul talks about these issues in a more personal way than in some of the earlier letters from Paul in the New Testament. You can imagine how you would write to someone whom you had worked alongside and felt very parental of. Paul also writes to Timothy with the urgency of an older man who wants to pour his years of experience into someone younger who can carry on the work.

IN CONTEXT

In his first letter to the Thessalonians, Paul reminded them that Jesus would come again to claim them and make a better world. Paul didn't know, though, that the church would take him sooooo literally. Some of them actually quit their jobs so they could watch for Christ. Others just started hanging out, looking for Christ's return. Still others got scared that Jesus had already come and they had been left behind.

SCRIPTURE BITS

Now the overseer [church leader] must be above reproach, the husband of but one wife, temperate, self-controlled, respectable, hospitable, able to teach, not given to much wine, not violent but gentle, not quarrelsome, not a lover of money.

1 Timothy 3:2–3

But godliness with contentment is great gain. For we brought nothing into the world, and we can take nothing out of it. But if we have food and clothing, we will be content with that.

1 Timothy 6:6–8

2 TIMOTHY

IN CONTEXT

Here's the scoop. . .

Written: *around A.D. 65*

Written by: *Paul, the apostle*

Writing style: *a personal letter*

One-liner: *Dear Tim, Come soon. I don't know how much longer I'll be here. Keep the faith!*

Final Instructions

Paul's second letter to Timothy is a poignant one. Paul knew that he was going to die soon. He was in prison. He had gone through several appeals. He knew that this was very possibly his last letter to Timothy, his last chance to tell him the things that matter.

It is a wonderful thing that this letter is a part of the Bible. We are made privy to the most significant thoughts of one of the most famous preachers in the history of the world.

What would you say to your son if you knew it was probably the last time you were going to be able to communicate with him? That's what the second letter from Paul to Timothy is all about.

Here are some of Paul's last words to Timothy, his friend and almost-son:

> *But as for you, continue in what you have learned and have become convinced of, because you know those from whom you learned it, and how from infancy you have known the holy Scriptures, which are able to make you wise for salvation through faith in Christ Jesus. All Scripture is God-breathed and is useful for teaching, rebuking, correcting and training in righteousness, so that the man of God may be thoroughly equipped for every good work. (2 Timothy 3:14–17)*

> *For I am already being poured out like a drink offering, and the time has come for my departure. I have fought the good fight, I have finished the race, I have kept the faith. (2 Timothy 4:6–7)*

TITUS

IN CONTEXT

Here's the scoop. . .

Written: *around* A.D. *65*

Written by: *Paul, the apostle*

Writing style: *a letter of instruction and training*

One-liner: *Dear Titus, Here are some helpful hints about leading your church.*

Follow the Leader

Titus was a young pastor in a very difficult parish. He was a pastor in Crete, a small island south of Greece. The people of Crete were known for their lies, their laziness, and their cruelty. It was a place that needed a church, but was it a place in which you could find any leadership for the church?

This was the challenge in front of Titus. It was also one of the reasons Paul wrote so much to Titus about the qualities of a leader. Most churches still use Paul's criteria today when they are choosing their leaders (pastors, deacons, or elders).

Here's how Paul believed leaders should behave:

For the grace of God that brings salvation has appeared to all men. It teaches us to say "No" to ungodliness and worldly passions, and to live self-controlled, upright and godly lives in this present age. (Titus 2:11–12)

But avoid foolish controversies and genealogies and arguments and quarrels about the law, because these are unprofitable and useless.
(Titus 3:9)

PHILEMON

Here's the scoop...

Written: *around A.D. 60*

Written by: *Paul, the apostle*

Writing style: *a letter of recommendation*

One-liner: *Dear Philemon, Forgive Onesimus not as a runaway, but as your brother in faith.*

Who Says You Can't Go Home Again?

Paul's letter to Philemon is a unique letter in the New Testament. It is simply a cross-sectional slice of life in the first century. The basic story is this: Philemon was a friend of Paul's. Philemon's slave, Onesimus, ran away and took some of Philemon's money with him. While Onesimus was wandering, he became a Christian and came in contact with Paul. After that, Onesimus decided to right his wrong and return to Philemon. Paul sent him back but with a letter hoping to soften Philemon's reaction. This book is that letter.

Basically Paul was calling in a favor. He reminded Philemon that he had received from life and it was time for the tables to turn. Here is Paul's logic:

Although in Christ I could be bold and order you to do what you ought to do, yet I appeal to you on the basis of love. (Philemon 8–9) [Paul appeals to Philemon's better self.]

So if you consider me a partner, welcome him as you would welcome me. (Philemon 17) [Paul appeals to their friendship.]

I, Paul, am writing this with my own hand...not to mention that you owe me your very self. (Philemon 19) [Paul is bordering on arm-twisting here!]

Confident of your obedience, I write to you, knowing that you will do even more than I ask. (Philemon 21) [You always know you'd better come through when the person asking the favor thanks you ahead of time.]

HEBREWS

Here's the scoop. . .

Written: *around* A.D. 70

Written by: *Paul, the apostle*

Writing style: *a letter to the New Testament Jews*

One-liner: *To all Jewish Christians. Now that Christ has come, focus on Him, rather than the rituals that pointed you to Him.*

When It All Began...

Back when the Jewish nation was young, Moses wrote down the laws for the nation as God told them to him. (See Exodus and Leviticus if you need a refresher.) Some of these laws were verrrrrrryyyy specific. As time passed and the Jewish people got more organized, some people made it their life's ambition to follow these laws. They concentrated so much on following the laws, that sometimes they missed the point of having faith in God: loving God and loving others. They were too busy following rules and regulations to do that.

When It All Continued...

Jesus spent much of His energies addressing this kind of issue. We still address it today. Some people say, "I don't consider myself religious, but I'm a Christian." This usually means they believe they follow the heart of faith instead of the head of faith, that to them it's not just a bunch of do's and don'ts.

When Will It All End?

Hebrews is addressing the same kind of thing. Some of the Jewish people were feeling like Jesus didn't make that much of a difference, that they could just keep following their laws and customs and that would make them righteous. The writer of Hebrews is saying to them, Jesus DID make a difference. He made all the difference. It's a whole different way of attaining righteousness—through faith in Christ, not in perfectly keeping the rules and making the sacrifices.

What You Find Out Along the Way

Hebrews gives some interesting insights into Jesus' role in our lives as a priest:

> But Jesus the Son of God is our great High Priest who has gone to heaven itself to help us; therefore let us never stop trusting him. This High Priest of ours understands our weaknesses, since he had the same temptations we do, though he never once gave way to them and sinned. So let us come boldly to the very throne of God and stay there to receive his mercy and to find grace to help us in our times of need. (Hebrews 4:14–16 TLB)

JAMES

Here's the scoop. . .

Written: *around* A.D. *50*

Written by: *James, probably the brother of Jesus*

Writing style: *a letter of instruction*

One-liner: *Yes, salvation is by faith, but faith without action is useless.*

Where the Rubber Meets the Road

If theology were a seesaw, you would put Paul's understanding of faith at one end and James' understanding of faith at the other. They were a good balance, but they came from different directions. Paul emphasized that we can't work or earn our way into God's good graces. We can only have faith and accept His grace. Paul wasn't saying that our faith is without responsibility. He was just saying that the responsibility comes out of having received the gift God offers. James came to it from the opposite direction. While he didn't contradict Paul, he pointed out that once we come to true faith, then our actions will be evidence of that faith. In fact James gave that as a guideline or a proof of faith, that true faith resulted in good actions.

Because of all that, James is a very practical book. It is a book that says not just what faith is, but what faith *does*. It is a book that explains not just what to believe, but how to live the life of a believer.

Even though James was probably written before Hebrews, it is a great book to come after Hebrews in the Bible. Hebrews is about faith. James is about faith applied.

James reminded his readers that being tempted and tested weren't the worst things that could happen to them. He reminded them that listening is not enough without action. He reminded them that how they treated other people would tell the most about what they believed. He reminded them that how they used their words mattered—a lot. He reminded them that the easy life wasn't always the most nurturing environment for faith.

In reminding them of all that, he reminds us as well.

THINK ABOUT IT THIS WAY

Q. As a Christian, how should I communicate?

A. *Everyone should be quick to listen, slow to speak and slow to become angry. (James 1:19)*

Q. What is the true test of our religion?

A. *Anyone who says he is a Christian but doesn't control his sharp tongue is just fooling himself, and his religion isn't worth much. (James 1:26 TLB)*

1 PETER

IN CONTEXT

Here's the scoop. . .

Written: *around* A.D. 60

Written by: *Peter, the disciple*

Writing style: *a personal letter*

One-liner: *These are difficult times. Let your faith help you endure. Don't let go just because troubles come.*

Finding Joy

Remember those movies where prehistoric TicketMaster sold tickets to Romans to go to the Coliseum and watch Christians face lions? The Book of 1 Peter was written about that very time. Christianity had even been outlawed! Anyone who claimed to be a Christian could be tortured, imprisoned, or even killed simply because he believed in God and believed that Jesus was God's Son.

You might think that if Peter was writing at such a volatile time, he would have been depressed or at least scared. You might think he would have written in code or revealed secret entrances to catacombs. When you read 1 Peter, though, you hear hope in Peter's message, not discouragement. You hear confidence and, if you listen really closely, you even hear joy. . . .

Praise be to the God and Father of our Lord Jesus Christ! In his great mercy he has given us new birth into a living hope through the resurrection of Jesus Christ from the dead. (1 Peter 1:3)

Therefore, prepare your minds for action; be self-controlled; set your hope fully on the grace to be given you when Jesus Christ is revealed.
(1 Peter 1:13)

But you are a chosen people, a royal priesthood, a holy nation, a people belonging to God, that you may declare the praises of him who called you out of darkness into his wonderful light. Once you were not a people, but now you are the people of God; once you had not received mercy, but now you have received mercy. (1 Peter 2:9–10)

The end of all things is near. Therefore be clear minded and self-controlled so that you can pray. (1 Peter 4:7–8)

That's an Interesting Point

Peter's first letter raises two interesting issues for us to consider. First, civil disobedience. When do we stop obeying the laws of our culture in order to obey God? Peter reminds us over and over to give respect to our government in every way possible. He doesn't give us easy permission to ignore the laws of our land.

Also, the issue of persecution in the face of our innocence. The people that Peter was writing to were not criminals. The thing they were being punished for was merely their faith. The sad truth of life is that we will face difficulties and mistreatment even when we don't deserve it. God's plan for us is not retribution. It is the ability to obey Him no matter what our circumstances. It is the ability to leave the "getting even" to God Himself.

2 PETER

IN CONTEXT

Here's the scoop. . .

Written: *around* A.D. 65

Written by: *Peter, the disciple*

Writing style: *a warning letter*

One-liner: *These are difficult times. Keep your faith and let it help you endure.*

Same Writer, Different Reason

Peter's second letter is to the same audience as his first letter. That audience is still facing difficult times. In this second letter, though, Peter is not only helping them combat enemies outside of the church. He was also addressing enemies inside the church: false teachers.

Evidently, Peter had heard that the false teachers were telling the church that Jesus wasn't REALLY coming back again and that they wouldn't REALLY be accountable for their actions. You can imagine the response. If I'm being persecuted for my faith and someone tells me that faith isn't really important, then what's the use? These false teachers were exploiting their listeners and misleading many, many people.

Different Reason, New Benefits

Because Peter was trying to "set the record straight" in light of false teaching, this short book has some of the New Testament's most bottom-line spiritual truths. It just works that way sometimes; you speak the most clearly when you are addressing a particular cause.

The Word of God: "Above all, you must understand that no prophecy of Scripture came about by the prophet's own interpretation. For prophecy never had its origin in the will of man, but men spoke from God as they were carried along by the Holy Spirit." (2 Peter 1:20–21)

God's nature: "The Lord is not slow in keeping his promise, as some understand slowness. He is patient with you, not wanting anyone to perish, but everyone to come to repentance." (2 Peter 3:9)

The second coming of Christ: "But the day of the Lord will come like a thief. The heavens will disappear with a roar; the elements will be destroyed by fire, and the earth and everything in it will be laid bare." (2 Peter 3:10)

The Christian life: "For this very reason, make every effort to add to your faith goodness; and to goodness, knowledge; and to knowledge, self-control; and to self-control, perseverance; and to perseverance, godliness; and to godliness, brotherly kindness; and to brotherly kindness, love. For if you possess these qualities in increasing measure, they will keep you from being ineffective and unproductive in your knowledge of our Lord Jesus Christ." (2 Peter 1:5–8)

THINK ABOUT IT THIS WAY

The truth is that Christianity has historically grown the most during times of persecution. Why? Partly because it is during those times that people face the truth rather than all the accessories that we apply to the truth. It's easy to give up a Family Life Center or a church softball league if you're going to face a firing squad. It's not so easy to give up the one hope you have that life is more than what we see in this world.

1 JOHN

Here's the scoop. . .

Written: *around* A.D. 90

Written by: *John, the disciple*

Writing style: *a letter of encouragement and instruction*

One-liner: *Ignore false teaching. Live righteously. Love each other. Know that Jesus was God in the flesh.*

Setting the Record Straight

In some ways, John wrote this first letter (that we call 1 John) to set the record straight. No sooner had the early church begun to organize itself than theological disagreements began.

"Maybe Christ wasn't really human," said one group.

"Maybe since Christ died for our sin, we don't have to try not to sin anymore," said another one.

John wrote to respond to these kinds of ideas. "Yes," he said, "Jesus was fully human and fully God. And yes, we must fight our sinful natures with everything we have, but when we fall, there is forgiveness."

John wrote to warn the people against heresies like these as well as the false teachers who spread their very unholy curricula. He also wrote to instruct Christians in the way of love. John reminded his readers that the very evidence of God's presence in us and with us is our love for each other. Some of the most famous verses about love in the Bible are found in 1 John.

This letter isn't a theological treatise, though. It's just thought after thought. It's sort of hard to outline, but it's a lot of truth in one place.

Dear children, let us stop just saying we love each other; let us really show it by our actions. It is by our actions that we know we are living in the truth, so we will be confident when we stand before the Lord, even if our hearts condemn us. For God is greater than our hearts, and he knows everything. (1 John 3:18–20 NLT*)*

Dear friends, since God loved us that much, we surely ought to love each other. No one has ever seen God. But if we love each other, God lives in us, and his love has been brought to full expression through us.
(1 John 4:11–12 NLT)

IN CONTEXT

John wrote one of the most well-known verses about the love of God in his Gospel. Usually if people only know one verse in the Bible, they know John 3:16: " 'For God so loved the world that he gave his one and only Son, that whoever believes in him shall not perish but have eternal life.' " Much of the Book of 1 John is an expanded form of this idea. In fact, John almost restates John 3:16 in 1 John 4:9: "This is how God showed his love among us: He sent his one and only Son into the world that we might live through him."

John was a man who had laughed and talked and traveled with Jesus. He was one of Jesus' best friends. He should know, better than just about anyone, how to explain God's love to us.

2 JOHN

Here's the scoop. . .

Written: *around* A.D. *90*

Written by: *John, the disciple*

Writing style: *a letter*

One-liner: *Keep your chin up and your hearts open, but keep a close watch on your faith.*

Hang in There!

The Bible isn't a book like an encyclopedia. It isn't just full of facts. It is the record of God's actions and people's reactions. Second John is a good example of the slice-of-life style of the Bible. It is a letter that John wrote either to an actual woman or to the church (using "lady" as a metaphor). It contains about the amount of words that would fit on one papyrus sheet of paper. It is a very personal letter like one you might write to a friend going through a difficult time. What would you tell him? You would tell him to concentrate on what matters. You would tell him to keep his chin up. You would tell him to listen to the right people. That's what John did.

Concentrate on what matters: "His command is that you walk in love." (2 John 6)

Listen to the right people: "Anyone who runs ahead and does not continue in the teaching of Christ does not have God." (2 John 9)

3 JOHN

IN CONTEXT

Here's the scoop. . .

Written: *around A.D. 90*

Written by: *John, the disciple*

Writing style: *a personal letter*

One-liner: *Keep up the good work! I'll be there soon to deal with the power struggle.*

On Problems in the Church. . .

John's third letter, like his second, could fit on one sheet of papyrus paper. This third letter was even more personal, though. It was addressed to Gaius.

This is what we know about Gaius—not much. There are four times the name Gaius is mentioned in the New Testament in association with the church, but we have no idea whether these are all the same man or not. We know from this letter, though, that THIS Gaius was much loved and valued by John. We know that he was hospitable to traveling preachers such as John and the apostle Paul. We know that Gaius was helpful. We can pretty easily assume that Gaius was a good person who was committed to following God and doing good things. He was the kind of person we would like to be.

John wrote to Gaius because of a power struggle that had risen in Gaius's church. (Already?! In the first century there was a power struggle in the church!?!) Evidently Diotrephes had been placed (maybe by John) in charge of the church. Later, though, when John sent people back to check on the church, Diotrephes wouldn't allow them to visit. John promised Gaius that he would come and deal with the situation soon.

It must have been as difficult to deal with church problems from a distance as it is to deal with them face-to-face today.

I could have no greater joy than to hear that my children live in the truth.

3 John 4 NLT

JUDE

IN CONTEXT

Here's the scoop. . .

Written: *around* A.D. 90

Written by: *Jude, probably one of Jesus' brothers*

Writing style: *a letter of warning*

One-liner: *Watch out for people who use God's grace as an excuse for irresponsibility!*

I Won't Stand for It!

If you had to describe the tone of the Book of Jude and if your only choices were

1. a party-type tone
2. a business-type tone
3. an intense, big brother type tone. . .

you would definitely choose #3: an intense, big brother-type tone. Jude had something to say and he expected everyone to listen and to take it as seriously as he did.

Truthfully, what Jude said WAS serious. He had spotted people who were destroying what God had created in the early church. He wrote this book as if to say, "Not on my watch." Not only did these people teach false doctrine, they destroyed fellowship, they deceived others, and used people for their own means. They basically said that now that God had paid the price for sins, it didn't matter what anyone did. They threw morals to the wind and encouraged everyone else to do the same.

It seems that almost every heresy is a distortion of the truth. If they were out and out lies, they would be much easier to spot. This heresy took a good thing, God's grace, and made it into a bad thing, a lack of responsibility to keep sin out of our lives. Jude wouldn't stand for it. Obviously.

SCRIPTURE BITS

Jude in a Nutshell

*Live in such a way that God's love can bless you as you wait for the
eternal life that our Lord Jesus Christ in his mercy is going to give you.
Show mercy to those whose faith is wavering.*

Jude 21–22 NLT

PROPHETIC BOOK

Revelation is the only book of prophecy in the New Testament. Most of it is a vision that John (the disciple) had while he was in exile on an island called Patmos. A lot of people consider Revelation a difficult book to understand. You can see why when you consider this: It's a description of heaven recorded by someone living in a world that has never even seen a video and hardly any special effects. Trying to describe another dimension with only the first-century world as a comparison? It's a stretch. But stretching is what John did, and in this book we have a picture of some pretty amazing stuff.

REVELATION

Here's the scoop. . .

Written: *around* A.D. *95*

Written by: *John, the disciple*

Writing style: *a prophetic vision*

One-liner: *This is how it will all work out in the end of the world as we know it.*

The End of the World As We Know It

The bulk of the Book of Revelation is about the end of the world, the apocalypse. In case you haven't noticed, a lot of people have spent a lot of energy preparing for, talking about, studying about, and just generally trying to figure out the details of the end of the world. One of the reasons it is so intriguing is that when the Bible talks about it, it is always in figurative language. It almost feels like a puzzle sometimes. While the Bible tells us Jesus will return like a thief when no one expects it, somehow we can't keep from trying to figure out just exactly when He'll return.

We have to remember, though, that the important thing about the "second coming of Christ" and the end of the world as we know it is the reminder to live each day honorably and connected with God, so should this be our last day, it is a good one.

The Seven Churches

Before John's Revelation went into its wilder end-times images, Jesus gave simple messages to seven churches through John. For most of the messages Jesus gave both an affirmation and a warning. Here's a quick review of those messages:

The Church at Ephesus:

You do the right things: you hate evil, you work hard, you persevere. But you've lost your first love. Put some heart back into your obedience. (Revelation 2:1–7)

The Church at Smyrna:

These are hard times for you and they are going to get harder. Be faithful and remember that your suffering won't last forever. (Revelation 2:8–11)

The Church at Pergamum:

You've remained true to God in an evil place, but you have not rid yourself of your evil influences. In this way you leave yourself at risk. (Revelation 2:12–17)

The Church at Thyatira:

You do many good things, but you let the people who teach lies continue to teach. How can you stand by and do nothing? (Revelation 2:18–29)

The Church at Sardis:

Wake up! You are so lifeless. You have a few people who are true to me, but you are a zombie as a church. I need you to pay attention. (Revelation 3:1–6)

The Church at Philadelphia:

You have been faithful. Keep persevering and I will protect you.(Revelation 3:7–13)

The Church at Laodicea:

You are complacent. You are hanging there in the middle. I'd rather you be hot or cold than just lukewarm like you are. (Revelation 3:14–22)

Special FX

After Jesus gives His charges to the churches, the rest of Revelation reads like a special effects display (or a sci-fi thriller, though this is certainly not fiction). John is in the midst of a vision of a whole different dimension than the one in which we live. He uses earthly images and language to give us as close a description as is possible. But how possible is it, really, to describe heaven in the language of earth? This is one of the main reasons why Revelation is so intriguing and yet so difficult to understand.

Basically, the end of the world will be a time when evil makes a last bid for people's allegiance through world leadership. There will be attempts to control our food, our loyalty, and our very survival and it all will be somehow connected to where we place our faith. This is a big reason why people of faith get so uptight when the government tries to control their behavior in terms of their religious beliefs.

A Revelation Glossary of Terms

There are many different opinions about the order of the last events of our world. But most agree that there will be these common elements: An evil power will rise that eventually demands that the world worship him. Jesus will take believers from the earth. There will be some kind of brand or mark that will be required for people to buy or sell. There will be a great battle between Jesus and the evil world leader. Jesus will win and

THINK
ABOUT IT
THIS WAY

If you like to read the last page of a book first, then Revelation is for you. In the great war between God and evil—God wins. That makes every day look a lot better.

Satan will be defeated permanently. Then we will all give account for our lives.

Here are some terms you might have heard along the way.

666: We don't know exactly how this number will be used, but Revelation 13:18 does say that the number of the "beast" (part of the evil power-head) will be 666. While no one is sure how the number will be used, everybody from movie producers to survivalists seem to know it's a number to stay away from.

Antichrist: The New Testament uses this term sometimes to mean any false teachers who try to influence people away from Christ, but in Revelation this term applies to a certain very powerful leader, probably with a political platform, who will be in power for three and a half years. He will eventually require the world to worship him and then will be defeated by Christ Himself.

Armageddon: The place of the final battle between Christ and the Antichrist, between good and evil.

Heaven: Revelation promises a new heaven and a new earth. Heaven will be our home when the world as we know it is over and gone.

Last Judgment: This is when we will face God and give account for our lives. At this point it will matter most whether we have trusted Christ's death to cleanse us from sin or whether we have mistakenly (and foolishly) trusted our own goodness to do that.

Millennium: A millennium is a thousand years. *The* millennium in Revelation is the thousand years that Jesus will reign in peace. There are differing opinions as to *when* this millennium will happen in the order of "end-times" events.

Rapture: This is the one-time event when Jesus will immediately call all Christians home to heaven. Sometimes this term is used interchangeably with "the second coming of Christ."

Tribulation: This term refers to a time of terror and trouble for believers on earth. Some people believe this seven-year period will happen before Christ returns and the rapture occurs. Others believe it will happen after that.

EPILOGUE

There's a lot of information in these pages, a lot of facts and numbers, a lot of details and stories. That's because the Bible is a lot of different stuff. It's not written like a novel with a beginning, middle, and end presented in a linear fashion. Instead it is slices of life lifted from people who connected with God and experienced Him.

It's not enough to just know the details. It's about knowing God. The point of the Bible, the power of the Bible, is that God's Spirit speaks to us through it if we'll read and listen. Yes, even though most of it was written in a barbaric time of humanity. Yes, even though our understanding struggles with some of the concepts. Yes, even though we sometimes come to it with so many misconceptions that we don't always give it a chance. Yes, even though it still includes some mysteries.

There is power in the Bible, because God is in it. It is His outstretched hand. We can read it for the sake of information, but that's not why it was written. It was written for the sake of a connection between God and us. It was written so that we would know the lengths He has gone to for us to believe in Him and be His children. It was written so that we could know Him.

The best way to read any book is to open the book, then to let the book open something in you. Open the Bible, and when you do, open your heart and let God speak to you.

It is relevant. To your life. Today.

Lists & Stuff

FINDING TOPICS THAT INTEREST YOU

There are a lot of resources these days that will help you find topics in the Bible. A lot of recently published Bibles have lists in the back. There are also books in the bookstores that are full of these lists to accompany your Bible. We've included a list here, just to get you started.

Abortion . . . . .Psalm 139; Isaiah 49:1–5

Adultery . . . . .Exodus 20:14; Proverbs 6:28–32;
Matthew 5:27–28; John 8:3–11

Anger . . . . .Psalm 145:8; Proverbs 29:11; Ephesians 4:25–32

Answered prayer . . . . .Matthew 21:21–22; Philippians 4:6;
Colossians 4:2; James 5:15

Bible . . . . .2 Timothy 2:15; Hebrews 4:12; 1 Peter 1:23–25

Church, Christ's body . . . . .1 Corinthians 12, 14; Ephesians 1:18–23

Contentment . . . . .Proverbs 19:23; Philippians 4:11–12;
1 Timothy 6:6; Hebrews 13:5

Crucifixion . . . . .Matthew 27; Mark 15; Luke 23; John 19

Death . . . . .Psalm 116:15; John 11; 1 Corinthians 15

Dependence on God . . . . .Jeremiah 17:5–8; 2 Corinthians 12

Depression, despair, discouragement . . . . .Psalm 42, 69; John 16:33

Drugs . . . . .Proverbs 23:29–35; Romans 13:11–14;
1 Corinthians 6:9–20; 1 John 3:7–10

Enemies . . . . .Exodus 23:4–5; Proverbs 16:7; 24:17; 25:21; 27:6

Faith in God . . . . .Genesis 15:4–6; Matthew 8:5–10; Luke 8:43–48;
Romans 5:1–8; Galatians 5:6

Family . . . . .Proverbs 5:18–21; 1 Timothy 5:3–5; 2 Timothy 1:5–8

Forgiveness for others . . . . .Matthew 18:21–35; Colossians 3:12–14

Forgiveness from God . . . . . . .Psalm 130:1–6; Ephesians 1:3–8; 1 John 1:9

Friendship . . . . .Proverbs 17:17; 19:4; 22:24; 27:6; Ecclesiastes 4:10

Guidance from God . . . . .Psalm 25:1–5; Psalm 139:1–10

Guilt . . . . .Psalm 32:1–5; 1 John 3:18–20

Healing . . . . .Psalm 103:2–5; Hosea 6:1–3; James 5:15–16

Heaven . . . . Luke 15:3–10; John 14:1–4; Philippians 3:18–20;
Hebrews 8:3–5; Revelation 21:10–27

Holy Spirit . . . . .John 16:5–15; Acts 2:1–4; Romans 5:1–5;
1 Corinthians 6:18–20

Homosexuality . . . . .Leviticus 18:22–29; Romans 1:18–27;
1 Corinthians 6:9–11

Hope . . . . .Psalm 25:1–3; 147:7–11; Romans 5:1–5

Humility . . . . .Proverbs 11:2; Philippians 2:1–9; James 4:6–10

Integrity . . . .Psalm 25:21; Proverbs 11:3; 1 Corinthians 15:33; Titus 2:6–8

Jesus Christ . . . . .Romans 3:21–26; Ephesians 1:3–14

Love of God . . . . .Romans 5:1–8; Ephesians 2:4–10; 1 John 4:7–12

Marriage . . . . .Genesis 2:18–24; Proverbs 6:27–35;
Matthew 19:3–6; Ephesians 5:21–33

Materialism . . . . .Matthew 4:8–11; 19:21–30; Colossians 3:1–2

Mercy of God . . . . .Isaiah 55:6–7; Micah 7:18;
Ephesians 2:4–8; 1 Peter 2:9–10

Money . . . . .Proverbs 15:27; Matthew 6:19–21; Mark 10:21–24;
1 Timothy 6:6–10

Parenting . . . . .Proverbs 13:24; Ephesians 6:4

Partying . . . . .Ecclesiastes 11:9; Matthew 24:42–51

Peace .Psalm 3:4–5; Romans 5:1; Philippians 4:4–7

Perseverance . . . . .Romans 5:3–5; Hebrews 10:36; James 1:2–4

Praise . . . . .Psalm 9:1; 47:6–9; 1 Peter 2:9

Prayer . . . . .Matthew 21:21–22; Mark 11:22–25; Luke 11:5–13;
Colossians 4:2

Repentance . . . . .2 Chronicles 7:14; Romans 2:4; 2 Corinthians 7:8–10

Resurrection . . . . John 11:25; Philippians 3:7–11; 1 Peter 1:3

Second coming of Christ . . . . .1 Corinthians 15:50–56;
1 Thessalonians 4:13–5:6

Self-worth . . . . .Psalm 139

Sex . . . . .Song of Solomon 5; Hebrews 13:4

Success . . . . .Proverbs 3:5–6; 21:30; Ecclesiastes 11:6; Micah 6:8

Temptation . . . . .1 Corinthians 10:13; Hebrews 4:15; James 1:13

Worship . . . . . .Exodus 20:2–4; Psalm 95:6–7; 100:1–5; Hebrews 12:28

FINDING HELP WHEN YOU NEED IT

WHEN YOU'RE. . .

Tired . . . . .Psalm 23

Hurting . . . . .Hebrews 12

Tempted . . . . .Daniel 1; James 1; 1 Corinthians 10

Needing some courage . . . . .Joshua 1; Ephesians 6

Needing some good advice . . . . .Proverbs

Depressed . . . . .Psalm 42

Struggling with right and wrong . . . . .Matthew 5–7; Colossians 2

Wondering who Jesus was . . . . .John 6–10

Trying to figure out the church .1 Corinthians 12

Feeling offended by someone . . . . .1 Corinthians 6

Finding it hard to believe . . . . .Hebrews 11

Needing to forgive someone . . . . .Philemon

Discouraged . . . . .Romans 8

Afraid . . . . .Psalm 27

Feeling like giving up . . . . .2 Timothy 2

Happy . . . . .Psalm 95

Wishing you hadn't said something . . . . .James 3

Struggling to do what's right . . . . .Romans 7–8

Not sure you're worth anything . . . . .Genesis 1; Romans 4, 5

Wanting to be closer to God . . . . .John 3

Feeling guilty . . . . .1 John 1, 2; Psalm 51

Lonely, left out . . . . .Psalm 25

Trying to be more loving . . . . .1 Corinthians 13

Looking for God's will . . . . .Philippians 2

Looking for guidance . . . . .Psalm 25

Wondering about abortion . . . . .Psalm 139

Wondering if success will make you happy . . . . .Ecclesiastes

Wondering how to become a Christian .Romans 10

FAMOUS LISTS

There are several famous lists in the Bible. You've probably heard of most of them. For your quick reference, here they are plus a few you might not be so familiar with.

THE TEN COMMANDMENTS

1. You shall have no other gods before me.
2. You shall not make for yourself an idol. . . .
3. You shall not misuse the name of the LORD your God. . . .
4. Remember the Sabbath day by keeping it holy. . . .
5. Honor your father and your mother, so that you may live long. . . .
6. You shall not murder.
7. You shall not commit adultery.
8. You shall not steal.
9. You shall not give false testimony against your neighbor.
10. You shall not covet your neighbor's house. You shall not covet your neighbor's wife, or... anything that belongs to your neighbor." (Exodus 20:2–17 NIV)

THE BEATITUDES (FROM THE SERMON ON THE MOUNT, GIVEN BY JESUS)

Blessed are the poor in spirit, for theirs is the kingdom of heaven.
Blessed are those who mourn, for they will be comforted.
Blessed are the meek, for they will inherit the earth.
Blessed are those who hunger and thirst for righteousness,
for they will be filled.
Blessed are the merciful, for they will be shown mercy.
Blessed are the pure in heart, for they will see God.
Blessed are the peacemakers, for they will be called sons of God.
Blessed are those who are persecuted because of righteousness, for theirs is
the kingdom of heaven.

Blessed are you when people insult you, persecute you and falsely say all
kinds of evil against you because of me. Rejoice and be glad, because
great is your reward in heaven, for in the same way they persecuted the
prophets who were before you. (Matthew 5:3–12 NIV)

THE ORDER OF CREATION

First Day: *God called the light "day," and the darkness he called "night."*
And there was evening, and there was morning—the first day.
(Genesis 1:5 NIV)

Second Day: *So God made the expanse and separated the water under the*
expanse from the water above it. And it was so. God called the
expanse "sky." And there was evening, and there was
morning—the second day. (Genesis 1:7–8 NIV)

Third Day: *The land produced vegetation: plants bearing seed according to*
their kinds and trees bearing fruit with seed in it according to
their kinds. And God saw that it was good. And there was
evening, and there was morning—the third day. (Genesis
1:12–13 NIV)

Fourth Day: *God made two great lights—the greater light to govern the day*
and the lesser light to govern the night. He also made the stars.
God set them in the expanse of the sky to give light on the
earth, to govern the day and the night, and to separate light
from darkness. And God saw that it was good. And there was
evening, and there was morning—the fourth day. (Genesis
1:16–19 NIV)

Fifth Day: *So God created the great creatures of the sea and every living*
and moving thing with which the water teems, according to
their kinds, and every winged bird according to its kind. And
God saw that it was good. . . . And there was evening, and
there was morning—the fifth day. (Genesis 1:21–23 NIV)

Sixth Day:	*Then God said, "I give you every seed-bearing plant on the face of the whole earth and every tree that has fruit with seed in it. They will be yours for food. . . . God saw all that he had made, and it was very good. And there was evening, and there was morning—the sixth day. (Genesis 1:29–31 NIV)*
Seventh Day:	*By the seventh day God had finished the work he had been doing; so on the seventh day he rested from all his work. And God blessed the seventh day and made it holy, because on it he rested from all the work of creating that he had done. (Genesis 2:2–3 NIV)*

THE FRUIT OF THE SPIRIT

But the fruit of the Spirit is

• *love*	• *patience*	• *faithfulness*
• *joy*	• *kindness*	• *gentleness*
• *peace*	• *goodness*	• *self-control*

Against such things there is no law. (Galatians 5:22–23 NIV)

THE ARMOR OF GOD

Therefore put on the full armor of God, so that when the day of evil comes, you may be able to stand your ground, and after you have done everything, to stand.

Stand firm then, with the BELT OF TRUTH buckled around your waist, with the BREASTPLATE OF RIGHTEOUSNESS in place, and with your FEET FITTED WITH THE READINESS THAT COMES FROM THE GOSPEL OF PEACE.

In addition to all this, take up the SHIELD OF FAITH, with which you can extinguish all the flaming arrows of the evil one.

Take the HELMET OF SALVATION and the SWORD OF THE SPIRIT, which is the word of God.

And pray in the Spirit on all occasions with all kinds of prayers and requests. With this in mind, be alert and always keep on praying for all the saints.
(Ephesians 6:13–18 NIV)

THE DESCRIPTION OF LOVE

> *Love is patient,*
> *love is kind.*
> *It does not envy,*
> *it does not boast,*
> *it is not proud.*
> *It is not rude,*
> *it is not self-seeking,*
> *it is not easily angered,*
> *it keeps no record of wrongs.*
> *Love does not delight in evil but rejoices with the truth.*
> *It always protects,*
> *always trusts,*
> *always hopes,*
> *always perseveres.*
> *Love never fails.*
>
> *(1 Corinthians 13:4–8* NIV)

SEVEN THINGS GOD HATES

There are six things the LORD hates,
seven that are detestable to him:
  haughty eyes,
  a lying tongue,
  hands that shed innocent blood,
  a heart that devises wicked schemes,
  feet that are quick to rush into evil,
  a false witness who pours out lies
  and a man who stirs up dissension among brothers.
(Proverbs 6:16–19 NIV)

THE FAMOUS "FOR EVERY THING" LIST FROM ECCLESIASTES

There is a time for everything,
and a season for every activity under heaven:
  a time to be born and a time to die,
  a time to plant and a time to uproot,
  a time to kill and a time to heal,
  a time to tear down and a time to build,
  a time to weep and a time to laugh,
  a time to mourn and a time to dance,
  a time to scatter stones and a time to gather them,
  a time to embrace and a time to refrain,
  a time to search and a time to give up,
  a time to keep and a time to throw away,
  a time to tear and a time to mend,
  a time to be silent and a time to speak,
  a time to love and a time to hate,
  a time for war and a time for peace.
(Ecclesiastes 3:1–8 NIV)